MEDIA SANS FRONTIERS

A 21ST CENTURY CRITICAL READING

EDITORS- DR. IRENE L | INDIRA N | DR. LALREMRUATI K& DR. DHEERAJ K

Contents

Preface

A few decades ago, every Sunday, family and friends would gather to watch programmes such as Mahabharata and evening movies. All that has now undergone a sea change. Technology has disrupted this pattern and along with it the culture of watching together. Viewers, now have the liberty to choose and watch from a plethora of genres from several different OTT platforms and that too at one's own convenience. It is no surprise then that the OTT media has grown by 30% in the number of paid subscribers from 22.2 million to 29.0 million between March and July 2020 (IBEF, Knowledge Centre, 2020).

The established players such as Netflix, Amazon Prime Video and Disney+ are facing stiff competition. A large number of other OTT players are set to disrupt and diversify the market with their innovations and contents. Also, the flourishing and growing multi-crore industry seems to be challenging the very survival of cinema halls and traditional media platforms such as cable or satellite television. The Data Sciences Division of Dentsu Aegis Network (DAN) India, in a report on the popularity of the OTT services in India, finds that "Binge Watching" as a culture is on the rise as a result of boredom particularly among Gen Z (ETBrandEquity, 2020). Also, Indians spend more time watching videos on the go and OTTs are eating into their travel and sleep time. According to the 'State of Online Video 2020' report by Limelight Networks, Inc., Indians spend on an average 11 hours (10 hours and 54 minutes to be precise) per week watching videos online whilst the global average is 8 hours (7 hours 55 minutes) (Sheth, 2020). The same report also finds that price is one of the major factors in consumer decision making and as per the report, 46 per cent of Indian viewers, said that they will cancel a streaming subscription due to high prices. This is in line with the global figure of 47 per cent. Price i.e. subscription is going to be the main issue. For a country like India, with a diverse population and demographics, contents too need to be right. The OTT platforms and the producers of the web shows are turning their attention to the choice of targeting family audiences.

Accumulation of 'soft power' is in any case costly, difficult, and time consuming. Solid reputations are only made over years. 'Soft power' has its drawbacks, though: it constrains as much as it enhances power. 'Honour' a term much used by governments of yore – dictated unpalatable political choices by excluding e.g. the possibility of compromise. As many an actor knows, furthermore, image is very constraining. The public expects behaviour in conformity with the image – sudden deviance may lead to severe loss of image. Coherence too, however, may be treacherous – solidity may be perceived as boring. The key factor is the availability of an alternative. There may be a smouldering dissatisfaction with the situation, but no overt revolt against it. As soon as people have a choice, they may exercise it.

Like a river, says Nye, a country's image has many sources. Only a few are under direct government control and amenable to deliberate enhancement. Whether states should enhance their image – spend to strengthen their 'soft power' – is an issue debated in the book, without clear outcome. In an ideal world 'soft power' would accumulate automatically through good and convincing deeds – anything else is 'propaganda'. Visions of crude manipulation by Nazis or Soviets come to mind. But convincing others of one's worth might need some pro-active doing. And in any case as any post-modernist intellectual might cynically interject – there is no truth, just opinions. So what's wrong with pushing a favourable opinion?

Editors
November, 2022

About The Editors

Dr. Irene Lalruatkimi

Dr. Irene Lalruatkimi is an Associate Professor in the Department of Mass Communication at Mizoram University, Aizawl, Mizoram, India. She is also heading the department since 2019 and she got her PhD from Assam University, Silchar, Assam. Prior to join here, she has worked as Assistant Director (Documentation & Publicity) at Mizoram State AIDS Control Society, Coordinator (Media Cell) for Sarva Shiksha Abhiyan (SSA), Mizoram and Assistant News Editor and News Stringer at Doordarshan Kendra, Aizawl Station. She has completed a major research project titled "Changing Media scape in Mizoram – A study of Social Factors Impacting the Professional Role Performance of Media Persons" has presented papers in the national and international conferences. She has also published research papers extensively.

Ms Indira Devi Nongmaithem

Ms Indira Devi Nongmaithem is an Assistant Professor in the Department of Mass Communication, Mizoram Central University, Aizawl, Mizoram. She completed her Post graduate from University of Hyderabad. She was heading the Department of Mass Communication, Mizoram Central University during 2017-2019.

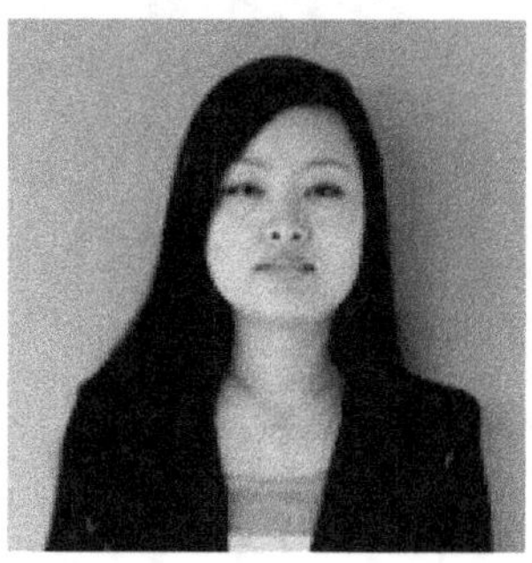

Dr. Lalremruati Khiangte

Dr. Lalremruati Khiangte is an Assistant Professor in the Department of Mass Communication at Mizoram University, Aizawl, Mizoram, India. She has been teaching in the Department for twelve years. She specializes in New media, Media laws and ethics and Video production. She has organized many seminars and invited lectures in the Department and has presented numerous papers in national and international seminars over the years. She has also been invited regularly for special lectures on media by other Departments and different local NGO's. She also contributes regularly to different programmes organized by the University as committee member. She is also one of the interview board members at DDK, Aizawl. She is also the creative director of the Annual Puppet Show that the Department organizes every year to different school kids around the University community.

Dr Dheeraj Kumar

Dr Dheeraj Kumar is an Assistant Professor in the Department of Mass Communication, Mizoram Central University, Aizawl, Mizoram. Previously he has worked as Assistant Professor in IIMT Group of Colleges, Greater Noida (Affiliated to Chaudhry Charan Singh University, Meerut) from July 2017 to Feb 2021. He has also worked as Guest Faculty at Makhan Lal Chaturvedi National University of Journalism and Communication, Bhopal, Madhya Pradesh from July 2015 to May 2017. He got his PhD in Electronic Media & Mass Communication from Pondicherry University (A Central University). Dr Dheeraj Bagged Best Teacher Award for Outstanding Performance and maintaining high standards in the field of academics for the session 2018-19 at IIMT College, Greater Noida (Affiliated to CCS University, Meerut). He has also received "Pt. Ram Pratap Bhatt Patrkarita Shikshan evam Shodh Samman" a State Level Award for special contribution in the field of Media Education and Research.

ONE

Challenges and Prospects of Regional Over-the-top (OTT) Platform: A Case Study on 'Darbu'

Joel Laltlanchhuaha
   Research Scholar , Department of Mass Communication
   Mizoram University: Aizawl, Mizoram.
   joeltlanchhuaha@gmail.com
   &
Dr. Irene Lalruatkimi
Associate Professor and Head,
Department of Mass Communication, Mizoram University.
irenevarte@gmail.com

Abstract: The media industry simulates an oligarchical organization with few corporations dictating the pace and pattern of our digital consumption. In this technological age, few media and technological companies controls our online content consumption in general, and our music appreciation in particular. In terms of musical content, digital streaming service providers like YouTube (Music), Spotify, and Apple Music, monopolizes the industry by acquiring most of the audiences through their mobile applications (Apps). In this paper, we conduct a case study on a regional local artists-based streaming platform in Mizoram 'Darbu – Music and Audio App'. Beginning its business adventure on 20th May 2022, Darbu already registered almost 1000 artists under its platform. The aim of this paper is to understand how the local faces the global, and how Darbu addresses the challenges from inside and outside the organization. We conducted six in-depth interviews with two representatives from Darbu and four local artists under them. We highlighted the issues and concerns of local artists and their overall experiences with the platform. Even though Darbu is a novice in the field of digital music streaming services, it envisages a rather optimistic future and manages to do quite well for now. However, it still has a long way to go to compare itself to other more mature players like YouTube and Spotify.

Key Words: *Darbu, Music, OTT platform, Digital Media, Streaming*

Introduction

The media sector mimics an oligarchy where a small number of firms control our digital consumption's speed and pattern. Few media and tech firms in this era of technology govern our online content consumption in general and our love of music in particular.New digital and social media channels have emerged, changing society in many ways and, in some situations, making traditional media less helpful (Kumar, 2021). Because of the progressive changes in media and technology throughout the last century, researchers refer to this world as being in the "post-performance" period (Thibeault, 2012). One of the best examples of how an innovation may completely disrupt an industry and render outdated established industry expertise is the quick transition of the music industry. The capacity to manage physical distribution was a major factor in the music industry's pre-Internet strength and influence. Physical music distribution is becoming less and less significant thanks to the internet, thus the established major music labels have to reinvent themselves to survive (Wikstrom, 2014).

The way we experience, make, and consume music has changed as a result of YouTube and other digital media. The majority of the industry's revenue today comes from digital music, and musicians are generally expected to maintain a presence online.Edmond (2014) went into detail about how music (videos) has migrated from television to the internet and how it has become a crucial component of YouTube.The YouTube effect has altered art, as well as other streaming services like Apple Music and Spotify. YouTube has had an impact on the musical art form, just like the phonograph, record player, cassette tape, CD, and digital audio file.The subscription economy and streaming service business have expanded quickly with the advancement of information technology. Particularly, the traditional music industry has been impacted by music streaming services. But very few attempts have been made to comprehend music streaming services in terms of general client satisfaction (Chung, 2022).Streaming, which was at first derided as the cuckoo on the nest of the music business, is now praised as the answer to declining CD sales and income losses due to piracy. In addition, the major labels are also receiving large payments from DSPs. However, the variety of the underlying contracts for streaming music and the combination of individual and collective agreements is perplexing and has greatly upset songwriters, performers, legal experts, and policymakers (Towsie, 2020).

We conducted a case study on the local "Darbu" digital music streaming OTT platform in this research. The study's main goal is to comprehend the opportunities and difficulties of running a streaming platform for regional musicians.The purpose of this article is to examine how regional apps respond to the problems brought by international behemoths like YouTube and Spotify.

What is an OTT platform?

Over The Top platforms or simply OTT platforms are digital streaming platforms that provide curated content directly to their users via the internet. OTT bypass traditional cable and satellite broadcasting and act as sole controller and distributor of their content. There is no globally accepted definition of OTT services, so governments, regulatory authorities, international agencies and other forums accept varying definitions depending on the context before them (Menon, 2022). Telecom regulatory authority of India (TRAI), in their consultation paper on Regulatory Framework for OTT services, defined OTT providers as 'a service provider that offers Information Communication Technology (ICT) relying on the global internet and access network speed (ranging from 256 kilobits for messaging to speeds in the range of Megabits (0.5 to 3) for video streaming) to reach out to the user by going "over-the-top" of TSP's network'. Further based on the service provided, TRAI classified OTT apps into three categories: Messaging and Voice services; Application ecosystems (mainly non-real-time), linked to social networks, e-commerce; and Video/audio content providers. Among these three categories, video streaming services like Netflix, Amazon prime etc., popularly described by the acronym OTT platforms in India.

The Emergence of OTT Platforms

During the 15 years that has passed since Napster was launched, the music industry has been completely transformed and the model that ruled the industry during most of the past century has been largely abandoned. According to a report in 2015, digital music brings in 55% of music industry revenue, 20% from physical sales, 15% from television and radio and 10% from public performances (FICCI-KPMG Report, 2015). The recent technological developments with the emergence of information and communications technology (ICT) and the Internet, simultaneously affects both of the competitive advantages of the major players: distribution and promotion.When it comes to advertising, ICT and the Internet have paved the way for consumer-to-consumer advertising through automated "recommender systems" (algorithms) and "online word of mouth" (Moreau, 2013).The changes brought about by the digital revolution in information and communication technology were highlighted by Cayari in 2011. In her theory, media had evolved from a passive to an interactive form, and these new multimedia formats would provide users greater control over how they consumed information and media. In addition to taking on a new shape, these new mediums and technology also make it possible for art to be consumed, produced, and shared in unprecedented ways.

Existing theories in social science about mass communication and interpersonal communication are insufficient to explain how new or digital media, which combines the traits of the two models, is developing quickly (Schroeder, 2017). Digital media have displaced and complement traditional media, especially among younger people. Schroeder (2017) asserts that new media enable both a scaled-up and more active media engagement by people. On the one hand, new media enable a more differentiated and fine-grained push of media towards audiences. Moreau (2013) analyses the cultural lag faced by major recording companies on the introduction of new technological developments; how digital platforms like Napster, YouTube, Spotify, etc., forced the institutions of music and the companies in re-structuring their business model, reluctantly ('technological discontinuity' or 'disruptive innovation'). He also discussed the process of 'dematerializing' music and the decline of 'star system' which was once an effective strategy of the labels.According to Daniel (2019), the CD is both a cultural artefact from the 1990s and a technological advancement that paved the way for a number of other disruptive advances in the music business. Radio broadcasting appeared to be a very successful marketing tactic for recorded music prior to the arrival of the digital age. Legend has it that the Decca record label "invented" the "star system" in 1929 by extensively promoting the works of a chosen group of its performers (Moreau, 2013). Today, it seems like YouTube will take over the radio's former role in that context.

OTTs and the Music Industry

The involvement of digital service providers (DSPs) or platforms that offer streamed music, such as Spotify, Apple Music, and Tidal, has fundamentally changed how copyright management organisations (CMOs) function and how songwriters and recording artists are compensated. Platform economics, which is used in this article to discuss music streaming services, has arisen from the economic analysis of two- and multi-sided markets. It offers new insights into how business is performed in the digital domain.Unlike past agreements, when the royalty paid to songwriters and performers was a proportion of sales, the financial model for music streaming is different. Payment for music streaming services is dependent on both subscription and ad-supported free service earnings.Towsie (2020) discusses these various strands with a view to understanding royalty payments for streamed music in terms of platform economics, offering some data and information from the Norwegian music industry to give empirical support to the analysis.Edmond (2014) charts the evolution of music video culture over the past two decades as well as the shifting significance of video music for musicians, viewers, and record companies in the modern YouTube era. He went into detail on how YouTube has included music (videos) and how it has moved from television to the internet. Digital aggregators like YouTube have ushered in a new music culture that is known for its "searchable, on-demand characteristic of Internet browsing."

The rise of the internet and social media platforms has revolutionized how bands establish themselves. Many of the same tactics like playing live, recording and distributing music, and seeking label attention remain the same; however, we've found that social media evens the playing field and empowers artists. By comparing three studies that specifically looked at YouTube music, Liikkanen&Salovaara (2015) trace the dominance of musical content on the platform and the contribution of the digital medium to the transformation of the music business. They also study the differences in viewing and listening patterns between music and other content genres on one hand and between different types of music videos on the other. They discovered that YouTube has been heavily used by people for musical purposes.

The market for streaming services and the subscription economy have expanded quickly with the advancement of information technology. The traditional music industry has been particularly affected by music streaming services. However, Chung (2022) argued that there haven't been many attempts to comprehend music streaming services in terms of general client happiness.Customer satisfaction, he found, is significantly impacted by all environmental elements, certain pricing-related factors, and content-related factors. Furthermore, the factors that determine satisfaction vary depending on the service.Conclusions drawn by Christensen (2022), following his research on the aftermath of Warner Bros-YouTube blackout, imply that the widespread use of streaming has increased demand for live events. The evidence is also in line with a differentiated Bertrand model of ticket pricing, in which prices are complementary from a strategic standpoint and where prices and streaming penetration result in growing variances in the artist profit function. This shows that concerts by other artists are alternatives for performances by a particular artist, whereas concerts by that artist's peers are complements in terms of demand.

Yessenbayev (2021) tries to show how designing music apps with a specific user group in mind can enhance the user experience. The bright neon colours and the "party aesthetic," which were at odds with their target audience's preference for peaceful music, were the elements of Apple Music's visual design that alienated the target demographic. Also, they discovered discrepancies between the anticipated functionality of a music streaming software and the capabilities that are already there. Arguing that there hasn't been much research on the recommendations made by music streaming services in the context of the entire system itself, Barackskay (2022) analysed the recommender systems of five prominent digital applications company. He found that although YouTube Music provided the most varied recommendations, the recommenders' perspectives were consistent among the other four sites. Customers' opinions of the recommendations made by their music service varied; they ranged from wanting no recommendations to praising the algorithm for introducing them to new music.The majority of the research done by Towsie (2022) has focused on the streaming music industry's supply side. The study prompts the fundamental query: to what extent can the music industry's long-term business strategy of streaming support the production of new works in a healthy music market? He argued that the music industry might be absorbed by a multi-product corporation, losing its uniqueness and perhaps any last claim to creativity. The economics of streaming, true to its reputation as the gloomy science, does not promise a bright future for the music business.

Rationale of the Study

We argue that the media sector mimics an oligarchy where a small number of firms control our digital consumption's speed and pattern. Digital streaming services like YouTube (Music), Spotify, and Apple Music dominate the market for musical material by drawing most of their users to their mobile applications (Apps). However, due to the multi-nationality of these platforms and its complicated service rules and policies, following the algorithms and trends of such platforms can become quite challenging for artists and audiences from less technologically equipped countries and regions. Even though, platforms like YouTube, Spotify and Apple Music provides a larger stage (audience) for relatively less popular artists, mostly regional, to showcase their talents and artistry, it is still arguable that these developments change the lives and careers of locally brewed artists and performers in the most significant manner.

'Darbu – Music and Audio App' is a regional over-the-top platform which emerges in the Mizo music scene recently. It is a music and audio application where audiences can buy musical contents (songs) of their favourite artists and stream them with a minimum price of Rs. 15 only. The rationale of this research is to understand the business model of 'Darbu' app and the challenges faced by the company executives in order to make it a profitable enterprise for artists, audiences and themselves. The general purpose of this research is to examine how regional apps respond to the problems brought by international players like YouTube and Spotify, and also how it seeks to address the problems and discrepancy that persists between international OTTs and local artists.

Objectives

a. To study the business model of 'Darbu' and the internal and external challenges faced by the enterprise as a content aggregator.
b. To study the effects of having regional OTT platform and how it impacts the musical career of local artists.

Research Questions

1. How do Darbu function as an OTT platform? What are the issues and challenges, both internal (management, piracy, audience retention, etc) and external (from other OTTs), that Darbu encountered as a creative enterprise?
2. What is the reception of Darbu by local artists? Does it have significant impacts in their musical career or experiences?

Methodology

This research follows an exploratory approach in qualitative social science research. The exploratory nature of our research found its basis on the novelty of both OTT platforms in general and the resulting lack of scientific study (and thereby existing literature) in the proposed research area. The study employed case study method due to the availability of only one regional OTT platform (dedicated to musical contents) in the research area and the peculiarity of having such platforms in a relatively small area (geographically and demographically) and, also, in the presence and dominance of global giants like YouTube and Spotify.

For data collection, we conducted six in-depth interviews with two representatives from LailenConsulting, the parent company of 'Darbu – Music and Audio App', and four local artists registered with Darbu. The two representatives from Lailen consulting were interviewed in their work office in Tuikhuahtlang, Aizawl. At the end of the interview, we acquired the phone numbers of some artists registered with them for further data collection. However, due to their busy schedule we could not conduct face-to-face interview with them. Therefore, we conducted in-depth interviews of the said artists via phone call. Before conducting these interviews, we prepared an interview schedule which contains some of the important points which should be covered while questioning. The data collected were analysed manually (no software employed) and categorised based on the requirements of the research objectives.

Findings and Discussion

The subject of our research is a relatively young enterprise with a business operation of merely more than four months (since May 20th 2022). Being such a novice in the music streaming market, it might seem quite unfair to challenge its projects and endeavours with international players like YouTube and Spotify. Nevertheless, for the purpose of this study we wanted to put this regional audio OTT platform on a pedestal and conduct a quasi-comparative study based on the foundations and business model framed by earlier platforms who offer the same service. The peculiarity of this OTT platform, Darbu, and therefore the reason for our investigation, is that unlike other similar service providers like Spotify and YouTube Music, our subject is concerned with and dedicated to local artists and musicians. It becomes intriguing to determine whether this regionality is a vice or a virtue for the company. Due to the exploratory nature of this case study, the findings of our research is less likely to be adequate to generalise the overall nature of the research subject, or the extent of its impact in the music industry of the research area i.e. Mizoram.

The Story of Darbu

Although there have been some initiatives to develop a platform for musicians and artists to market their creative products before, Darbu (Music and Audio App) is arguably the first systematic, incorporated, and successful platform for musical contents in the state of Mizoram. Commencing its business journey on 20th May 2022, Darbu envisage a promising future as regional artists and musicians cried for a systematic process for reasonable capitalization of their hard labour in writing a song or delivering a creative melody. After the end of cassette tape era, artists in Mizoram, and possibly other parts of the world, can no longer find a worthy alternative to market their creative products. Rina, Head of Business Development (Darbu), said, "In Mizoram, there were neither apps nor websites where musicians could sell their songs. Songs were once purchased on CDs and cassette tapes. The only resource the singers have now is YouTube. Additionally, few artists in Mizoram receive enough views due to the small population for them to support themselves as professionals" (Lalrinnunga, personal communication, Sept 23, 2022). He added that it was Darbu's mission to address this issue and that the love of music is the primary force behind the creation of such platform.

The term "darbu" refers to a Mizo musical instrument made up of three brass gongs that is used in ceremonial dances. The goal of the music streaming service is to help singers get paid what they are due. Listeners can purchase an album for Rs 150 and a song for Rs 15 through the app. An artist could sell their album on Darbu and make the same amount of money if 200 people buy it as opposed to getting around Rs 30,000 for a million YouTube views (Colney, 2022). Till date, Darbu application have 20,867 users or downloads through Play Store (Google) or App Store (iOS) and registered almost 1000 artists from inside and outside (non-resident Mizo) Mizoram. The application is administered by 7 personnel which comprises of music enthusiasts, media professionals and technical experts provided by Lailen Consulting, the parent company of Darbu. Their business model is simple but effective. Artists can sell their new releasesin Darbu Exclusive and get 90 percent cut from the total revenues, which is credited to their linked bank account at the beginning of the month, for the previous month. They can also showcase their already released songs for streaming and sell their merchandise on the same platform. When releasing new songs, artists are advised (Darbu and artists verbal agreement) not to put their songs in other platforms like YouTube, Spotify, Apple Music, etc. and only make it available on Darbu for digital purchase for at least one or two months. "This is to boost the digital sales so that artists can have handsome rewards for their creative works. It'sfor the benefit of the artist and the artist only", said Alan, Chief Executive Officer of Lailen Consulting (Alan, personal communication, Sept 20, 2022). They also added that their original business plan is to run advertisements in their platform and reward artists for the number of streams their songs have on the same. However, this will only be achievable when the platform acquires "a considerable number of users". They intended on doing this by expanding their platform beyond just music streaming and include other contents like audio book and other audio files. In a sense, Darbu as a music OTT platform is like a child who is learning to walk. Step-by-step the developers of the platform are learning, experimenting, and expanding the scope of Darbu to be the most influential development in the history of Mizo music industry.

Challenges of Moderating Regional Music OTT

In an era where international superstars like Spotify, YouTube (Music), and Apple Music dominate the digital streaming industry, it is inevitable and rather obvious that running a regional platform that offers the same service is accompanied by many challenges both inside and outside of the company. The (un)availability of resources in terms of skilled labour and financial and or capital sanctions has been one of the major concerns in a small populated geography like Mizoram. When asked about the initial reception of Darbu by local artists sand audiences, Rina, the Head of Business development of Darbu app, told the interviewer that there was some "scepticism on the part of the artists" and added that this was not unexpected as artists often fall victim to various scams and fraudulent schemes during their musical career (Lalrinnunga, personal communication, Sept 23, 2022). Also, almost all of the artists that we interviewed told us that they came to know of Darbu by direct word-of-mouth from one of the developing team of Darbu app. Stacy, one of the most powerful and prominent gospel singer in the state, told the interviewer that she was introduced to Darbu by one of the executives of Lailen Consulting (the parent company of Darbu) who also happens to be her friend (Stacy, personal communication, Sept 20, 2022). The other artists that we interviewed are also closely acquainted with the developers of Darbu application. Darbu representatives also told us that they organized semi-formal familiarization program with local artists group like Mizo Domain Mizoram (MDM) and Mizo ZaimiInsuihkhawm (MZI) in order to inform their members of the project and missions of Darbu app. These organizations are also registered later in the platform to showcase the songs and renditions of their respective members. However, there has not been any formal program or campaign to advertise the platform on a large scale.

The Darbu team is comprised of seven core members with different expertise. The technical aspect of which is mostly provided by Lailen Consulting who appointed other members of the development team in terms of the requirements of the journey. When asked about the availability of technical staff and experts needed for the company, Mister Alan of Lailen Consulting replied, with a rather unsatiable fervour, that the resources they have was sufficient for their current project, hinting the need for more technical expertise and experiences if they should expand and continue the business project further. Another technical issue faced by Darbu, and arguably every other music streaming platform, is the problem of piracy. During its short business journey of a little over four months, Darbu experienced a copyright violation of around ten instances. The most recent one is the case of Kimkima, one of the most celebrated artists in the state, who had his song pirated and streamed on YouTube by the perpetrator. "On the first four days of releasing my song on Darbu, the sales amounted to Rs. 40,000 approximately; by that pace I had hoped to reach Rs. 1 lakh in sales in a month. But then it was pirated and streamed on YouTube. Since people can listen to it for free on YouTube my sales on Darbuslumped significantly. I was devastated. Nowadays, the cost of producing a song is high...it was catastrophic", Kimkima recalled the incident (Kimkima, personal communication, Sept 21, 2022). The perpetrator had been apprehended and a court case is on-going for this incident. This kind of issues has always been one of the major challenges of running an OTT platform in general. So, it is likely that Darbu will also face similar issues in its future and, therefore, it becomes imperative for the developers to address it as effectively as possible.One of possible challenges of running content aggregation platform is the problem of payment. The business model of buying songs per song could be a major challenge in the pre-net-banking or Google Pay era. This has been one of the major downfalls of earlier attempts of producing online platform for music buying. One example is Mizo Store, an online music market which was introduced in the beginning of the 2010s. "One of our biggest challenges was the online payment process", Mister Alan, who is now the Chief Executive Officer ofLailen Consulting, told the interviewer. He added that Darbu was launched at a perfect time as the general population familiarized themselves with online payment methods and other technical know-how needed for the app to be successful because of the pandemic. However, the original business plan was to stream music based on subscription and run ads to generate revenue, much like other available platforms. They also plan to incorporate social networking features on the app to make it more engaging and interactive for users.

In order to capitalize their audience artists are advised to share their new songs exclusively on Darbu for at least one to two months before sharing it to other platforms or intermediary services like Distrokid. The company executives also said that revenues from music sales alone would not suffice the needs of the organization even if they take hundred per cent of the profit. In order to promote their contents, the Darbu team created and used various social media accounts like Facebook, Twitter, and Instagram which are jointly managed.

The Impact on Local Careers

Till date, Darbu has registered a little short of 1000 artists under their platform; that is a remarkable number taking into account the platform has been up and running only for four months. From this statistic, it is evident that local artists are in support of the company's project and vision. However, due to this short period of business time, it is difficult to estimate exactly the impact of Darbu on local music scenes and how it will play out in the future. While conducting our interviews, most of the artists agree that Darbu will need time to adapt the the digital environment in order to make it a successful enterprise for all parties involved. Most of the artists interviewed hold a rather optimistic view of the app while mentioning the need to incorporate some necessary features (like copyright claim) for the app to survive the tough competitions from other global service providers.

All of the artists, except one, that we interviewed for this research informed us that YouTube was the first platform that they used to market and showcase their musical product. This indicates the influence of digital media in the music industry. YouTube in particular was one of the most influential developments not only in the media or music industry, but also for society in general. Previous studies in this area also found that many artists all over the world started their musical career in this digital stage and used is as a 'promotional tool' for their contents. Also, before and after Darbu was introduced, YouTube is the main source of revenue for many local artists, including our research subjects. Other sources of income includes live performances, sales of merchandise, and streaming revenues from other platforms like Spotify, Apple Music, and Amazon Prime. All of the artists that the researcher interviewed are either directly or indirectly (through mutual friend or acquaintance) related to the developing teams of Darbu. Consequently, most of them came to know of Darbu by offline word-of-mouth prior to its launching on 20th May 2022. The artists interviewed also reported that their revenue structure has not been drastically changed yet by the introduction of Darbu. However, this could be attributed to the novelty of Darbu platform to the general population. Nevertheless, our subjects are optimistic in terms of revenue generation once they supply more songs to the platform as some of them only published one or two songs on the platform. Even so, the sales record for these songs has been significant especially in the first few days or months.

From our interview, it is clear that artists are aware of the digital potential and the necessity to maintain an online presence in order to stay relevant. Our subjects use different social media platforms like WhatsApp, Instagram, Twitter and Facebook in order to reach different types of audiences. One artist told the researcher that Instagram is effective for reaching younger audiences while Facebook is good for its wider/global reach (Kimkima, personal communication, Sept 21, 2022). The other artists also agree that different platform is good for different types of audiences or demographics. While the majority of them seem to agree that Instagram and Twitter are the most relevant platforms, one artist claim that he got the best responses or reaction from WhatsApp activities. All but one artist that the researcher interviewed also reported that they use third party service called 'DistroKid' in order to market their songs. Founded in 2013 by American entrepreneur Philip J. "Pud" Kaplan, DistroKid offers digital distribution service to artist and musicians based on subscription. When artists subscribe to their service, their musical content gets distributed to various online music retailers like Spotify, Apple Music, YouTube Music, Amazon Music, Pandora, etc., whenever they make a new song and submit it to DistroKid. The reason for subscription is mainly ease of use and efficiency in related services like copyright claims.

One of the artists that the researcher interviewed praised Darbu for its content aggregation, especially its aggregation of old songs and classics for the audiences. One other said that Darbu addresses the life-long issue of the public by making it easy to buy their favourite songs from their favourite artists. Nevertheless, they are also full of suggestions to make Darbu a more useful and successful business endeavour for both artists and audiences. Copyright problems, small number of users, and the presence of more advanced and more equipped platforms (YouTube, Spotify and others) were the most common problems or issues that concerns the local artists. One artist hinted that the process of buying songs can be challenging for less technologically equipped audiences, while other artist said that the act of buying a song is kind of an out-dated practice and that some audiences can be reluctant to pay their hard-earned money on Darbu when they can listen the same song for free on YouTube.

Conclusion

From this research it is clear that running a regional music platform service is quite a challenging and daring business endeavour. Especially in an era where YouTube and Spotify the audio (and video) streaming market and acquire more and more users globally, regional artists-based platform like Darbu – Music and Audio App is a novice in the game, a child learning to take its first step. However, finding its origin from a casual conversation between two music enthusiasts in the summer of 2014 (Colney, 2022), Darbu has come a long way since then. Though the future of this novel app will surely be full of twist and turns, it is nonetheless a beacon of hope of many local artists who are in desperate need of a system that allows them to capitalize their musical labour. The main objective of our research was to explore the life experiences of this artistic creation from the perspective of the developers and the artists as well. Throughout our relatively short in-depth study, we set out to unveil the directions and movements of this app. Since the platform has only been in the business for just over four months, it is still difficult to generalize the nature of its business model and the potential it has to turn the Mizo music industry around. However, we believe that conclusions drawn from this research will provide new avenues for future research into the relationship between digital media and society in general, and between the music industry and digital streaming services in particular.

References

Airoldi, M. et al., (2016) Follow the Algorithm: An Exploratory Investigation of Music on YouTube. *Poetics.* http://dx.doi.org/10.1016/j.poetic.2016.05.001

Boyle, J.D., Hosterman, G.L., & Ramsey, D.S. (1981). Factors Influencing Pop Music Preferences of Young People. *Journal of Research in Music Education.*

Cayari, C. (2011). The YouTube effect: How YouTube has Provided new ways to Consume, Create, and Share Music. *International Journal of Education & the Arts*, 12(6).

Chandler, D., & Munday, R. (2011) *Dictionary of Media and Communication.* Oxford University Press.

Chen, K. (2019). Competitions Between OTT TV Platforms and Traditional Television in Taiwan: A Niche Analysis.*Telecommunications Policy.* https://doi.org/10.1016/j.telpol.2018.10.006.

Cherpoot, Z. &Laltlanmawia (Eds.). (2021). *Mizo Rap Music Zirchianna (A Critical Study of Mizo Rap Music).* Government Hrangbana College.

Christenson, P.G. & Peterson, J.B. (1998). Genre and Gender in the Structure of Music Preferences. *Communication Research.* https://doi.org/10.1177%2F009365088015003004.

ColdFusion. (2015) How Did YouTube Start, retrieved from https://www.youtube.com/watch?v=P4dT-lW9260, accessed on 04/03/21 @ 10:30 PM.

Colney, K. (2022). Why Darbu, Mizoram's First Music-Streaming App, Focuses on Musicians. *EastMojo.* https://www.eastmojo.com/mizoram/2022/07/23/why-darbu-mizorams-first-music-streaming-app-focuses-on-musicians/, accesed on 18/09/22 @ 10:00 PM.

Daniel, R. (2019). Digital Disruption in the Music Industry: The Case of the Compact Disc. *Creative Industries Journal.* DOI: 10.1080/17510694.2019.1570775

Dougan, K. (2014) YouTube Has Changed Everything"? Music Faculty, Librarians, and Their Use and Perceptions of YouTube. doi:10.5860/crl.75.4.575

Edmond, M. (2014) Here We Go Again: Music Videos after YouTube. *Television New Media* DOI: 10.1177/1527476412465901

Figueiredo, F. et al. (2014). Does Content Determine Information Popularity in Social Media?: A Case Study of YouTube Videos' Content and their Popularity. *Human Factors in Computing Systems*

Fleischer, R. &Snickars, P. (2017). Discovering Spotify – A Thematic Introduction. *Culture Unbound, 9*(2), 130-145.

Grenier, L. (1990).The Construction of Music as a Social Phenomenon: Implications for Deconstruction. *Canadian University Music Review*.

Hopper, J. (2018). Marginalization in the Music Industry: A Twitter Expose. *Routledge*

Housely, W. (2017). *Digital Society and the Sociological Imagination*. Cardiff University Press

Kumar, K. J. (2021). *Mass Communication in India*, (5th Ed). Jaico Publishing House.

Lange, P. G. (2008). (Mis)conceptions about YouTube. In G. Lovink& S. Niederer (Eds.), *Video vortex reader: Responses to YouTube*. Institute of Network Cultures.

LeBlanc, A. (1979). Generic Style Music Preferences of Fifth-Grade Students, *Journal of Research in Music Education*. https://doi.org/ 10.2307%2F3344712.

Lepa, S., Steffens, J., Herzog M. &Egermann, H. (2020). Popular Music as Entertainment Communication: How Perceived Semantic Expression Explains Liking of Previously Unknown Music. *Media and Communication, 8*(3), 191–204.

Li, S. (2017). Television Media Old and New: A Niche Analysis of OTT, IPTV, and Digital Cable in Taiwan. *Telematics and Informatics*. http://dx.doi.org/ 10.1016/j.tele.2017.04.012.

Lindlof, T. R., &Shatzer M. J. (1998). Media Ethnography in Virtual Space: Strategies, Limits, and Possibilities. *Journal of Broadcasting & Electronic Media, 42*(2), 170-189.

Liikkanen, L.A. &Salovaara, A. (2015). Music on YouTube: User Engagement with Traditional, User-Appropriated and Derivative Videos. *Elsevier Limited*. http://dx.doi.org/10.1016/j.chb.2015.01.067

Manolios, S., Hanjalic, A. &Liem, C. (2019). The Influence of Personal Values on Music Taste: Towards Value-Based Music Recommendations. *Thirteenth ACM Conference on Recommender Systems*. https://doi.org/10.1145/ 3298689.3347021.

McLuhan, M. (1966) This Hour Has Seven Days, Interview, Canadian Broadcasting Corp, YouTube Title – 'Marshall McLuhan 1966 – Predicting the

Internet with Robert Fulford', Interviewer – Robert Fulford, Retrieved from https://www.youtube.com/watch?v=ijeMM-NXvus, accessed on 05/03/21 @ 9:30 PM.

McLuhan, M. (1967). *The Medium is the Massage*, Penguin Group.

McQuail, D. (2010). *Mass Communication Theory* (6th ed), SAGE Publications India Pvt Ltd.

Menon, D. (2022). Purchase and continuation intentions of over -the -top (OTT) video streaming platform subscriptions: a uses and gratification theory perspective.*Telematics and Informatics Reports 5* (2022) 100006 https://doi.org/10.1016/j.teler.2022.100006.

Moreau, Francois. (2013). The Disruptive Nature of Digitization: The Case of the Recorded Music Industry. *International Journal of Arts Management.*

Nightingale, V. (2012). Media Ethnography and the Disappearance of Communication Theory, *Media International Australia.*

Palfrey, J., & Gasser, U. (2008). *Born digital: Understanding the First Generation of Digital Natives.* Basic Books.

Ridder, Sander De. (2013). Are digital media institutions shaping youth's intimate stories? Strategies and tactics in the social networking site Netlog. *New Media Society.*

Sadana, M. and Sharma, D. (2021), "How over-the-top (OTT) platforms engage young consumers over traditional pay television service? An analysis of changing consumer preferences and gamification", Young Consumers, Vol. 22 No. 3, pp. 348-367. https://doi.org/10.1108/YC-10-2020-1231.

Scott, J. (1994). *Dictionary of Sociology.* Oxford University Press.

Smelser, N.J. (1963). *The Sociology of Economic Life.* Englewood Cliffs.

Stafford, S.A. (2010). Music in the Digital Age: The Emergence of Digital Music and Its Repercussions on the Music Industry. *The Elon Journal of Undergraduate Research in Communications,* 1(2).

Thibeault, M.D. (2012). Music Education in the Post-Performance World. In G.E. McPherson & G.F. Welch (Eds.), *The Oxford Handbook of Music Education.* Oxford University Press.

Tlanghmingthanga, K. (1994). *Zorimawi: Music Ministry of the Mizos,* LTL Publications.

Traber, D.S. (2001). L. A.'s "White Minority": Punk and the Contradictions of Self-Marginalization. *Cultural Critique*

Wali, A. (2010). Ethnography for the Digital Age. *American Anthropologist,* 112(1), 147-148.

Wilson, B. (2006). Ethnography, the Internet, and Youth Culture: Strategies for Examining Social Resistance and "Online-Offline" Relationships. *Canadian Journal of Education, 29*(1), 307-328.

Wimmer, R. D., & Dominick, J. R. (2014). Mass Media Research: An Introduction (10th ed.). Cengage Learning India Private Ltd.

TWO

PREVALENCE OF OTT PLATFORMS AMONG MIZO MOBILE USERS

Author(s)

Vanlalchhanchhuahi[1] Dr. Junali Deka[2]

[1]*PhD student, Mass Communication and Journalism Department, Tezpur University, Napaam, Sonitpur, Assam 784028*
Email: tekokie11@gmail.com

[2]*Assistant Professor, Mass Communication and Journalism Department, Tezpur University,Napaam, Sonitpur, Assam 784028*
Email: junali4@gmail.com

Abstract

In spite of its geographical disadvantages and economic conditions, number of mobile users in Mizoram has significantly increased. According to Economic Survey (2020-2021) by the Planning and Implementation Department, Government of Mizoram, number of mobile connections during 2018-19 is 11,35,632 out of which 4,57,566 are Airtel users while 3,12,413 are Reliance Jio users, 2,05,835 are BSNL users and 1,60,088 are Vodafore/ Idea users. With the internet having its way among the general public by the early 2000s brought forth by BSNL which also started mobile internet (2G) connection by the year 2004, there has been an enormous growth in mobile internet connection the following two decades. The 2019 pandemic has apparently boosted Mizo software developers to create mobile applications in order to cater the need of Mizo mobile users including several OTT platforms. This paper looks into the consumption behaviour as well as benefits and drawbacks of Mizo OTT platforms among the users using survey questionnaires while case study is done on Mizo mobile applications like Lersia Play, Runmawi and Bawmrang TV which are the most popular apps (specifically) for streaming original Mizo movies and series. The Unified Theory of Acceptance and Use of Technology (UTAUT2)is employed to study how these applications are adopted and used by the consumers.

Keywords: Internet, Mizo, Mobile applications, OTT platforms, UTAUT2

Introduction

OTT "Over the Top" stands for any content delivery streaming service over the internet (Partap & Mittal, 2022), it can be any standalone, streaming content that uses the internet and goes beyond the distribution of traditional media platforms like cable TV or telecommunications networks (Layzell, 2020). OTT is a term used for those providers who distribute content/streaming media directly to viewers, through the Internet (MICA Report, 2019). OTT apps combine the reach and power of traditional TV without a cable box with the scale and flexibility of the internet to create an unstoppable dynamism for content creators, distributors, and brands all over (ibid). OTT Platformsallow you to pay for the type of content you want to watch without having to deal with a cable operator, satellite connection, or other broadcast channels (Khurana & Mehta, 2022).

Pervasiveness of individualism can cause a family to disperse, perhaps not physically but mentally, where each member can immerse in one's own choice of content without having to think of the other persons' preferences while enjoying their favourite piece with their favourite digital platform as Soares (2018) wrote that individualism posits that the primary unit of reality as well as the ultimate standard of value is an individual. The choice of an individual has become more important than what the others are interested in. Every family member, be it young or old, wishes to have their own smartphone where they can have maximum control or authority over it. In the midst of this, the idea of OTT platform seems to be quite apt where every individual can subscribe to his/her favourite app or content with ease. Not only children but also adults don't have to fight over TV remote control anymore as OTT platforms become a solution or a peacemaker. Fans don't have to wait for a certain timing to tune in to their much awaited shows, they can just buy/rent in a few click or tap at any moment at their own conveniences. This study tries to look into the prevalence of OTT platforms among Mizo mobile phone users while considering their consumption behaviour as well as the pros and cons of Mizo original OTT platforms. A case study will be done on three movie/series streaming platforms viz., *Lersia Play*, *Runmawi* and *Bawmrang TV*.

Rationale of the study

The concept of Over The Top Platform is quite new to the people of Mizoram and the existing OTT Platforms are also launched very recently. The earliest ones being released around the year 2021, this is a much unexplored area of study which will have a better scope in future as more platforms are launched with more variety of content. OTT platforms will also pave a way for the growth of film industry in Mizoram which is currently lagging behind when compared to other states in India.

Background of the study

Mobile internet connection is a fast growing business in Mizoram. The earliestconnection was provided by the Bharat Sanchar Nigam Limited (BSNL) in February 2004 led by BSNL, only GPRS internet was available initially (Lalawmpuia, 2021). 3G internet was introduced in 2012, upgraded to H+ in 2015 which was expected to offer the fastest speed possible in a 3G network. 4G network paved its way in 2019 allowing users to access the fastest available internet yet it covers only Aizawl - the capital city and district headquarters which has been expanding to other districts. Airtel reached Mizoram on 26th June 2006 and Reliance Jio in March 2015.

Objectives:

1. To find out the level of awareness about OTT Platforms among Mizo mobile users.
2. To study the existing Mizo OTT Platforms for movies and series.

Research Questions:

1. What are the factors effecting the adoption of OTT Platforms among Mizo people?
2. What are the pros and cons of the existing Mizo OTT Platforms?

Research Methodology

The research design is exploratory in nature where mixed methodology is employed for the study. Online survey is conducted among Mizo Mobile Users using Convenience Sampling Method and Case Study is done on Mizo

Original OTT Platforms (specifically movie and series streaming applications) viz. *Lersia Play, Runmawi* and Bawmrang TV.

Review of literature

MICA Report (2019) did an industry mapping and trend analysis on various OTT platforms like YouTube, Hotstar, JioTV & JioCinema, Voot, SonyLIV, Amazon Prime Video, Netflix, Zee5, Airtel TV, Hungama, ALTbalaji, YuppTV, Eros Now, TVFplay, Viu, MX Player, Ullu, ShemarooMe, Sun NXT, Hoichoi, Addatimes, OTT Watch List as well as several other platforms and found that OTT is progressively becoming stronger and the preferred type of content consumption through all demographics and opined thatin the coming years a large number of films will find direct-to-digital or post theatrical digital releases.They also mention that regional is the new battle zone as the leading global players have understood the regional taste and hence the upcoming platforms are going regional. The average revenue per user (ARPU) for pay TV is likely to decrease to four times that of OTT in 2020, from six times that of OTT in 2017. This report also mentioned that Telecom Regulatory Authority of India (TRAI) has issued Consultation Paper for OTT communication services regarding Regulatory Framework which is similar to Telecom Service Providers.

Khurana & Mehta (2022) in their work *OTT Platforms: A boon or Bane* wrote that India has a high chance of becoming the second-biggest OTT market (after US) to reach a value of ?138 billion by the end of fiscal year 2023. Some of the factors mentioned affecting adoption of OTT are high content qualityCost, Convenience, Content availability, User experience, Features, Smartphone and Mobile internet penetration and Net neutrality whichcause the increasing acceptance of OTTservices. Social distance during Covid-19 pandemic has boosted at-home digital use and increase the demand for streaming services where users enjoy the rewarding experience of content customization as well as watch history based customization.

Saha (2021) also stated that the future will have a lot more reliability over virtual platforms making shift in the customer touch-point where the global and national companies along with the regional ones have built different models for distributing content and generating revenues. The author also found that entertainment is the key factor that generates interest and draws attention to OTT platforms.

Ogbo et.al (2021) wrote that even though there has been a significant growth in OTT adoption in the African countries, there is shortage of empirical studies on the impact of OTT where the voice of consumers also remains underrepresented. They also talked about the debatable nature of net neutrality which could probably bridge the digital divide yet is less likely to be essential in developing countries as the restrictions made could hamper competition in the market.Their study also found that there is no increase in mobile phone adoption because of OTT arrival and there is a lower preference for OTT plans among women as compared to men.

Gomathi & Christy (2021) in their work *Viewer's Perception TowardsOTT'Platform During Pandemic* wrote that the internet has brought technological shift which brought along new kind of viewing experience where collective movie watching is replaced by a personalised or individualized viewing style. They also believe that the reasons behind the growth of OTT medium can be smartphone penetration rate, International partnerships between media entrepreneurs, quality of the medium, cost effectiveness as well as access liberty.

Theoretical Framework

UTAUT/UTAUT2

The Unified Theory of Acceptance and use of technology (UTAUT) was put forward by Venkatesh et.al (2003)(Ramirez-Correa et al., 2019) by revising, mapping and integrating constructs (Tamilmani, 2017) which comprises of eight models: the Technology Acceptance Model (TAM), The Theory of Planned Behavior (TPB), the combined TAM and TPB Model, The Motivational Model, The Theory of Reasoned Action, The Model of PC utilization, the Innovation Diffusion Theory, and the Social Cognitive Theory (Martinez & McAndrews, 2022). This accumulation of several research efforts described in different models and theories of Technology Acceptance is considered as an attempt to unify terminology of variables of different models and theories in Technology Acceptance (Ahmad, 2014). Built as a framework to study the method of understanding and accepting new technologies by users, how users can use, and what effect could continuing use have, it also tries to define that certain factors such as usefulness, ease of use, complexity, and social influence can affect the users' choice and use of technology (Momani, 2020). The modification of UTAUT modification (i.e, UTAUT2) added the three additional constructs, namely - hedonic motive, cost/perceived value and habit which are moderated by age, gender and experience and emphasize more on the private user segment, the behaviour along with consumer's technology acceptance to attain broader generalizability while,UTAUT was originally designed to study technology in organizational settings (Marikyan & Papagiannidis, 2021). The three added variables: hedonic motivation, price/value and habit play an important role in the use of new technologies by consumers (Arenas et.al, 2015). There has been an enormous increase during the last few years in the number of studies that use UTAUT2 in various context of technology adoption (Tamilmani et.al, 2017). UTAUT2 is an essential framework which plays an important role for the improvement and understanding of the adoption process of various technological phenomena such as M-banking (Farzin, et.al, 2021). Even though UTAUT has the highest clarifying capabilities for user intentions and usage behaviours among the existing models the ability of UTAUT2 is better than UTAUT to interpret users' adoption behaviour (Wu, et.al, 2022).

Findings and Discussion

Survey Findings

Online survey form was sent to more than 300 people using Convenient Sampling Method but only 17.3% (i.e. 52 respondents) have submitted. The main reason for this very poor response is because the population of the study generally find the topic a little daunting as they are not much aware of it which is also an evidence that there is a very little awareness about OTT platforms among Mizo Mobile users.

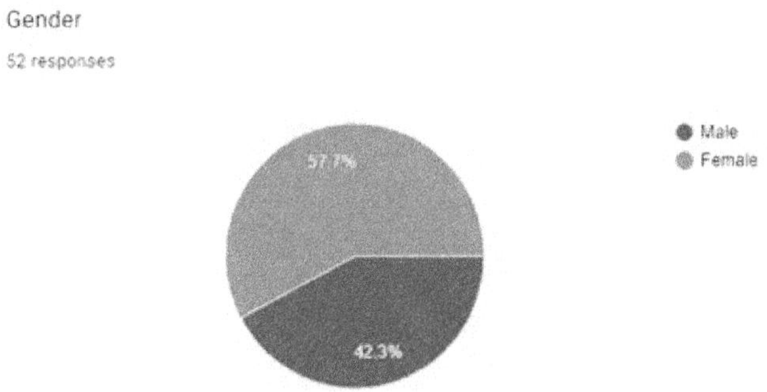

Out of 52 responses 57.7% i.e, 30 are Female and 42.3% .ie 22 of the respondents is male.

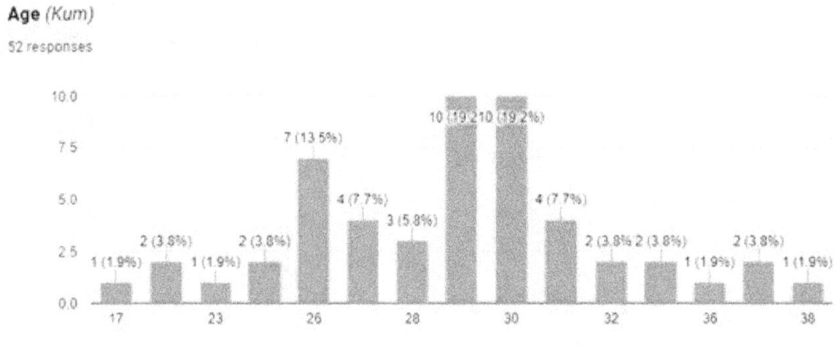

The average age of the respondents is 28 where mode is 29.5. The youngest respondent is 17 years old and the oldest is 38. The highest frequency in terms of age becomes 29 and 30 as 10 respondents (19.2%) each are of this age.

Smartphone user
Smartphone hmang
52 responses

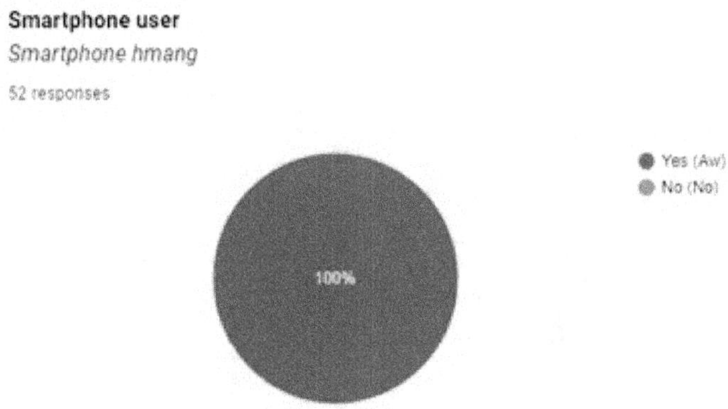

All (100%) of the respondents are Smartphone users which also proves that in spite of its geographical disadvantage, Mizoram has a high mobile penetration rate.

1. Are you aware of OTT (Over the top) platforms?
OTT (Over the top) platform i lo hre tawh ngai em?
52 responses

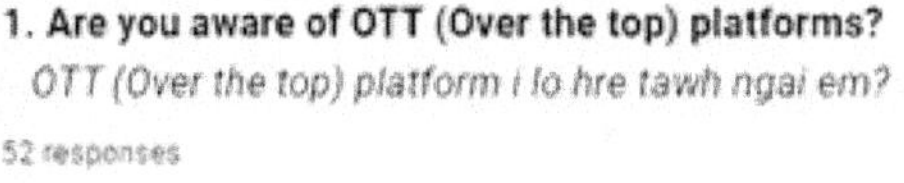

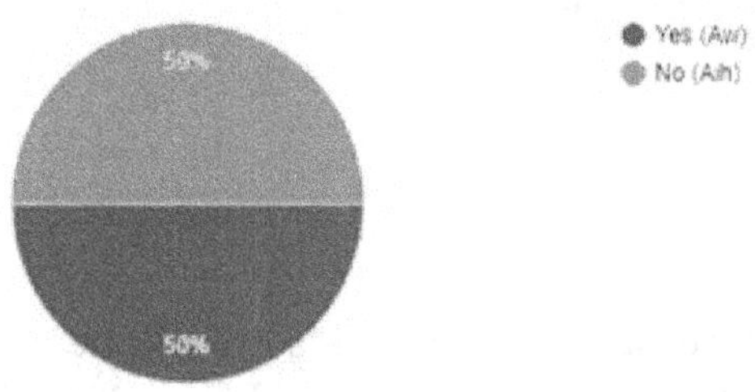

Half of the respondents (50%) are aware of the term OTT platform while another half (50%) are not. Some of the respondents mentioned that the term is not familiar with them yet when it is described or explained, they are familiar with it. OTT platform is a new term for many of the respondents which made a number of individuals in the population reluctant to respond to the survey fearing that they might make mistake which results in poor response to this survey.

3. Do you watch Mizo online movies/series via mobile apps?

Mizo movie/serial te mobile app hmangin i en thin em?

52 responses

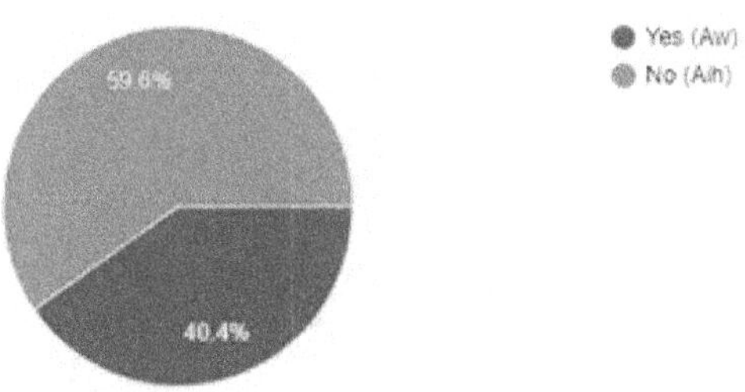

More than half (59.6%) of the respondents said they do not watch Mizo online movies/series using mobile applications. The main reason for this is that they are unwilling to spend money while the rest 40.4% of the respondents watch Mizo movies/series using mobile application.

4. Do online movies/series replace your TV consumption?

Online movie/serial i enin i TV en hun a luahlan em?

52 responses

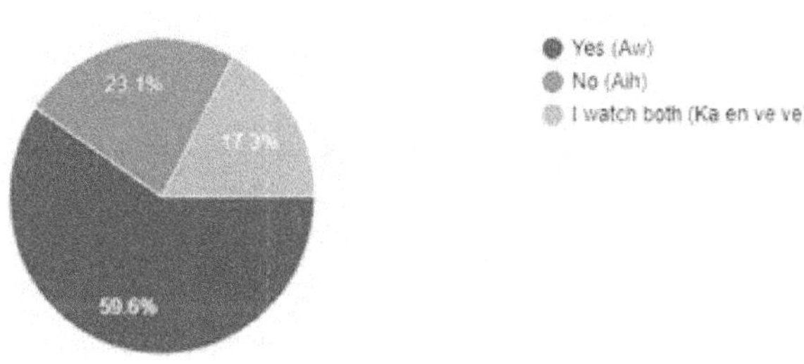

More than half (59.6%) of the respondents said that online content has replaced their living room TV consumption, while less than three-fourth (23.1%) of the respondents are still watching TV and the rest (17%) are using both conventional and new media without the other medium replacing another.

5. Do you rent/buy movies online?

Online-in movie i lei/hawh thin em?

52 responses

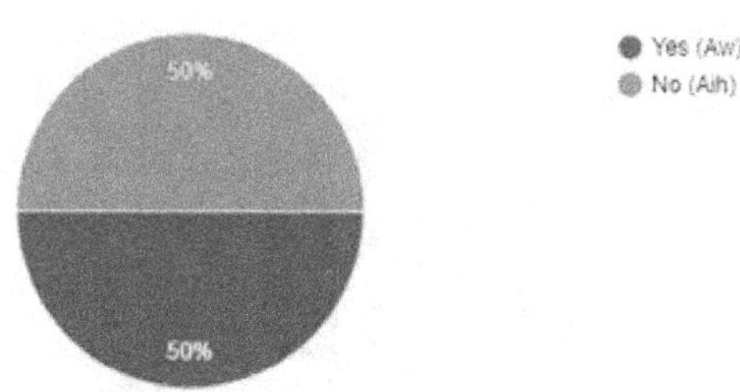

Half of the respondents (50%) do rent online movies and series while another half (50%) do not. This small sample size has equal distribution of online movie renters. Many of the respondents also consider it a waste of money to spend on such items.

6. How much time do you spend on online movies/series in one day?

Ni khatah engtia rei nge online movie/serial i en thin?

52 responses

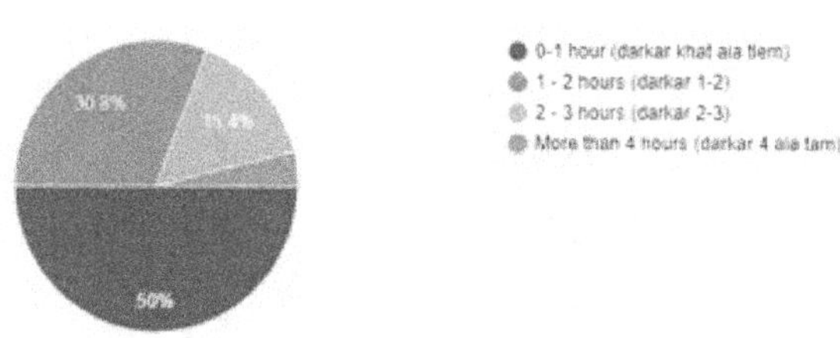

Half of the respondents (50%) of the respondents spend 0-1 hour watching online movie/series, almost one-third (30/8%) of the respondents spend 1-2 hours, only 15.4% of them spend 2-3 hours while a very few (3.8%) of the respondents spend more than 4 hours on online movie/series in one day. This shows that the rate of consumption is quite moderate - the reason in some areas can be poor internet connection.

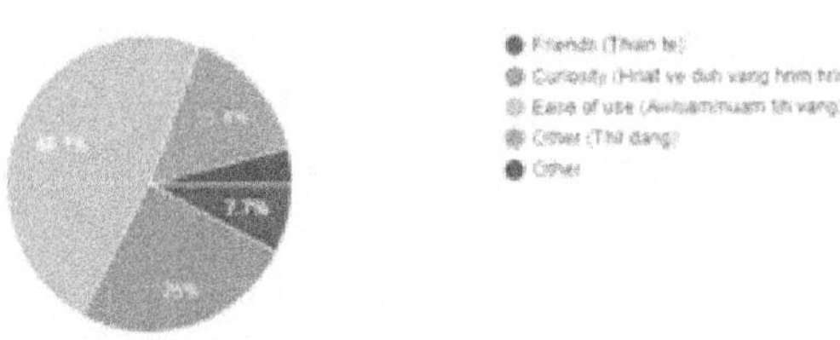

In terms of motivation/influence, almost half (48.1%) of the respondents said they use OTT platforms due to ease of use, less than one-third (25%) use because of curiosity while 29.2% of the respondents use because of other reasons and a very few (7.7%) of the respondents use because of influence of others/friends. It can be seen from here that the Mizo mobile users have the curiosity to explore and figure out various online platforms using digital devices. Other reasons mentioned include time pass, eagerness to see new movies, advertisements and shout-out(s) from social media platforms.

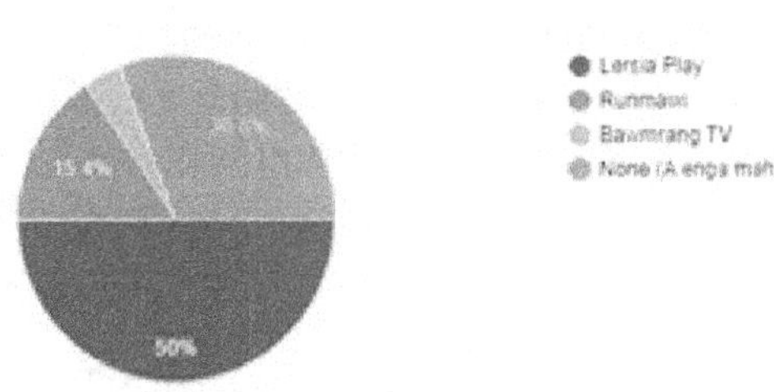

The most widely known app amongst the three Mizo OTT platforms is *Lersia Play* which is familiar to half of the respondents (50%), almost one-third (30.8%) of the respondents are not familiar with any of these apps. 15.4% of the respondents are most familiar with *Runmawi* app amongst the three while only 3.8% are most familiar with *Bawmrang Tv*. While many of the respondents(30%) are not familiar with none of these apps there are also who are familiar with all of them yet they are made to choose the most familiar one amongst the three OTT platforms.

Three open ended questions were asked at the end i.e. what the respondents like about Mizo Mobile Applications and what they don't and how Mizo OTT platforms can improve when compared with the global platforms 54% of the respondents said they don't have anything they like or don't like in particular since they are not using Mizo OTT platforms. Some of the advantages of Mizo OTT platforms mentioned include the support towards the achievement of having Mizo original applications (33% of the respondents) and also for promotion and development of Mizo movies and shows. The most common disadvantage mentioned include purchase duration, less variety or content, not user friendly; overpricing issues, access problem and poor customer support service.The respondents also suggested some ways in which Mizo OTT platforms can be improved which are - revision of pricing, password sharing policy, availability of wide genre, revision of the duration of time scale/rent period of paid movies, making it more user friendly and becoming more public service based than a profit based business, focusing more on reliability than market competition, longer subscription period, getting updated or upgraded according to the need of the market as well as adding more subtitles to Mizo content in order to reach wider audience.

Findings on Mizo OTT Platforms Case Study

Lersia Play

Lersia Play is one of the most successful mobile applications (OTT Platform) developed by Lailen Consulting Pvt. Ltd. The first Mizo OTT platform *Lersia Play* was launched in July 2021 by a joint collaboration of Lailen Consulting Pvt Ltd and Leitlang Pictures, an original Mizo Film Maker (Lalhriatpuia, 2022). The app was built with a willingness of running without profit (or even loss)for at least three years but they started gaining profit right from the fourth month. Many of their customers are from outside India but are Mizo.This platform currently has 24 movies - *Zalenna* (2020), *Norah* (Romance) 2021, *Scooty* (Romantic Comedy) 2021, *Khawnglung Run*(Historical Drama, Action) *2021, Nunna Thar*2021, *Tuirial Jail 2021, Laltheri*2021, *Duhaisam*(Romance) 2021, *Dengi I love you*(Romantic Comedy) 2021, *Kyhpachatupa na nei* (Romance) 2021, *Comrades* 2021, *Ka Bialnu*2021, *Emy* (Horror)2021 and *Call 112* (Crime) 2021. *Apate* (Horror) 2022, *Eleison Zahngai rawh*(Docudrama) 2022 with subtitles in English, Hindi and Tamil. *Depression Anxiety* (Faith based) 2022, *Thihna nen ni khat* (Horror, Comedy) 2022, *Driver Kima* (Comedy) 2022, *Saki* (Thriller) 2022, *Nukawki Pasal*

(Comedy, Drama), 2022, *Luoithli* (Romantic Action), 2022. *Lersia Play* has an original series *Bangla No. 9 (The truth behind the wandering soul)*with its 6th episode as the latest. Classic Mizo movies such as *Zothansangi* (2004), *Thamral si lo* (2004), *Ngurthansangi* (2004)*Luah Loh Lungdi*(2004), *Lenmawii* (2004), *Engtik niah emaw chuan* (2000), *Nicky Cruz* (2003), *Mission* (2004) and *House no. 109*(2002) are also available at Lersia Play app as well as Lersia.com.

Lersia Play developer Lailen Consulting Pvt Ltdwas started in the year 2018 with three key persons who are interested in software development. They have been freelancing since 2008 before they finally decided to set up their own firm. The CEO of the company used to take up part time job(s) in online software development companies during his undergraduate studies to ease the financial burden that his family had. His freelance experience helped him get acquainted with foreign clients and as he got in touch with people who have the same interest and passion, they agreed to collaborate and set up their own company, initially called *Dumde* in 2010. Even though he got the opportunity to work at Infosys, an Indian Multinational IT Company, he declined because he saw the condition of the software industry in Mizoram and his zeal to meet the need and demand of the state by the residents themselves has led him to start this company. Things didn't go as they expected since Mizo people in general are so use to getting software(s) free of cost. Most of the revenue was earned from foreign clients at first but in order to get more clients, they need manpower which is not an easy task as it is difficult to find locals with the required skills and knowledge. By the year 2013, the ICT Department under the government of Mizoram set up an e-governance society where they set up a big State Data Centre and the staff of this firm decided to apply for the available posts. They were all recruited and worked for 5 years. After having a good enough experience from the government sector, they came back to their senses as their passion for software development couldn't die. So, they all resigned from their government job and as they now knew how and where to tap, resulting in the launch of Lailen Consulting Pvt. Ltd. which is a pioneer IT Consultancy and Software Development company in Mizoram. As they became more aware of funding sources as well as available IT projects which can be taken up by a firm like theirs, they decided to run a private company yet partnering with the government while executing certain tasks. They have realized that many of the state government projects are undertaken by companies from outside Mizoram and as they have observed as well as validated some of the works done by various Indian IT companies while they are still in the government sector, they came to know that Mizoram need an IT firm which will work in partnership with the state government. With the estimation of having the same potential and skills that the external companies are showing, they march forward to meet the demand of the government as well as the public. Their main businesscore is software service.

They started making Mobile Applications with the intention of serving the needs of the society. They want to build trustand provide the needs of the people by allowing the public to use their applications at minimum cost. Their major achievement in this regard is creating mobile applications during the pandemic which help users get their work done using these applications from their home.

Runmawi & Bawmrang TV

*Bawmrang TV and Runmawi*apps are created by the same developer ATBuys Pvt. Ltd. but since the filmmaker partner for Bawmrang TV (which was launced in June 2021) decided to create only Gospel or Christian content, the developer launched another application called *Runmawi*in September 2021 for streaming more varied content so that they can reach wider audience (Lalremruata, 2022). The website of Bawmrang TV declared that their server is hacked and their mobile application is also not functioning at the same.

Runmawi is one of the flourishing OTT Platform in Mizoram streaming Mizo series, movies and live shows. The application was launched in September 2021 with three shareholders – Lalremruata Chhakchhuak, Zothangvunga and Lalengmawia. These Computer Engineers collaborated with Mizo Film makers, signing contract on a yearly basis. This annual partnership allows them to work with film makers. For the year 2022*Runmawi* has signed an annual contract with Mizo Film Forum.

Runmawi hosted Mizo Got talent (MGT) during October – November 2021 in order to help Mizo people in finding their talents as it provides entertainment to their users. This (MGT) event also helped in promoting *Runmawi*application as it attracts performers or participants as well as audiences from various part of Mizoram.

By September 2022),*Runmawi* has the following content: 14 Movies – *Master Hranga,*(Comedy)2021, *Tlan rawh,* (Short Movie) 2021, *Nutei Thingpui Dawr,* (Thriller)2021, *Biak In Ropui* (Kids Movie) 2008, *Thingtlang Tlangval*(Romance)2020, *Trampa* (Thriller) 2021 *Thian Lungdum* (Romance)

2021, *Mikhual Zaklo*(Comedy) 2022, *Ni khat Chauh* (Romance) 2022, *InspectorArina* (Comedy) 2022, *Tuizual Ngaw* (Thriller) 2022, *KA U Liana* (Mizo Story) 2022, *Hawrawp Hnuhnung Ber* (Thriller) 2022. 10 dubbed movies – Bounty Hunter (Korean) 2016, The Gifted (English) 2014), I fine thank you, love you (Thai) 2014, Pandora (Korean) 2016, Ghost Ship (English) 2015, Bad Genius (Thai) 2017, Hot Young Bloods (Korean) 2014, Midnight Runners (Korean) 2017, The Battleship Island (Korean) 201, I can Speak (Korean) 2017. Besides these *Runmawi* app had hosted a reality show called Mizo Got Talent (MGT) which is available in their app. This app also has its original series *Boss Amanda* and *Keimahni. Boss Amanda*, a crime serial was released on 113th May 2022 with 2 Seasons having 3 episodes each. *Keimahni*, claimed to be the first Mizo SitCom is *Runmawi's* original mockumentary which currently has 2 seasons with five episodes each. Most of the dubbed movies/shows are Korean.

Runmawi gets 30%-40% of the revenue earned from their app while 60% to 70% of the share goes to the Filmmakers or production partner(s) and the revenue earned so far is good according to the Managing Director, Lalremruata Chhakchhuak. The Director also said that the demand for good filmmakers and cast and crew is becoming high, not only who can but who are good in acting, videography, cinematography, script writing etc. As film making is not an easy task, unless skilled people are involved, a lot of energy and resources can get wasted. *Runmawi* has customer support/ helpline which is available to customers from 10 AM to 10 PM every day. In spite of its short existence, they said that their customers are fairly quick in adopting the technology although customers from rural areas are facing more difficulties than the ones in the city.

Conclusion

There is a very little awareness about OTT Platforms among Mizo mobile users as well as the people in general. Since OTT Platforms were launched in Mizoram only by the year 2021, there is not much to study yet but looking at the promising nature of it, it will be a good area of study in future for digital media scholars and film critics as well.Even though the benefits of OTT platform highlighted by some authors mentioned in the review of literature includes cost-effectiveness, easy accessibility etc., the OTT consumers in Mizoram mentioned that the available content are a little overpriced for them. Most of the movies/series are available for rent only for several hours which discourage many potential consumers to buy them. Due to shortage of streaming content in the available apps, the no. of hours spend on Mizo

OTT platform is quite less as compared to national and global platforms. The respondents are happy to have original Mizo OTT Platforms. As manyof the potential users are of the opinion that they will consider using Mizo OTT only when a single or regular subscription give access to all the content, developers also need to consider that in order to draw more customers. There is also negligence from the developers' side regarding their customer queries. Awareness or familiarity with the term "OTT Platform" along its usage will enable users in sharing their viewing experience and not shy away from sharing their consumption behaviour. The main hindrance to adoption of OTT platforms is the issue of the cost. As UTAUT is a framework to study the method of understanding and accepting new technologies by users, how users can use, and what effect the continuing use could have as and as it also tries to define certain factors such as usefulness, ease of use, complexity, and social influence can affect the users' choice and use of technology, the main factor affecting Mizo Mobile Users to adopt OTT platform is ease of use. Even as the Mizo OTT distributors said they earn good revenue from their business, steps can be taken to be more inclusive towards people from all economic background.

References

Arenas Gaitán, J., Peral Peral, B. y Ramón Jerónimo, M.Á. (2015). Elderly and Internet Banking: An Application of UTAUT2. Journal of Internet Banking and Commerce, 20 (1), 1-23

Farzin, M., Sadeghi, M., Kharkeshi, F.Y., Ruholahpur, H., & Fattahi, M. (2021). Extending UTAUT2 in M-banking adoption and actual use behavior: Does WOM communication matter? Asian Journal of Economics and Banking.

Gomathi, S., & Christy, N.V (2021). VIewer's Perception Towards 'OTT'Platform During Pandemic (with special reference to Coimbatore city). International Journal of Creative Research Thoughts, 9(8), 593-693.

Lalawmpuia, (2021). Face to Face Interview. BSNL SDEO.

Lalhriatpuia, A. (2022). Face to face interview. CEO. Lailen Consulting Pvt. Ltd.

Lalremruata, C. (2022). Telephone Interview. Managing Director, ATBuys Pvt. Ltd.

Layzell, C. (2020). OTT Trends & Future Predictions. Zemoga Newsletter.

Marikyan, D. & Papagiannidis, S. (2021.) Unified Theory of Acceptance and Use of Technology: A review. In S. Papagiannidis (Ed), TheoryHub Book. http://open.ncl.ac.uk

Martinez, B. M., & McAndrews, L. E. (2022). Do you take...? The effect of mobile payment solutions on use intention: an application of UTAUT2. Journal of

Marketing Analytics, 1–12. Advance online publication. https://doi.org/10.1057/ s41270-022-00175-6

MICA Report (2019). Indian OTT Platforms Report. New Regional Flavours, More Entertaining Content. The School of Ideas. Centre for Media & Entertainment Studies.

Momani, A. (2020). The Unified Theory of Acceptance and Use of Technology: A New Approach in Technology Acceptance. International Journal of Sociotechnology and Knowledge Development.

Ogbo, E., Brown, T., Gant, J., Davis, A., & Sicker, D. (2021). The Impact of Over-the-Top Services on Preferences for Mobile Services: A Conjoint Analysis of Users in Nigeria. Journal of Information Policy, 11, 403–443.

Ramírez-Correa, P., Rondán-Cataluña, F. J., Arenas-Gaitán, J., & Martín-Velicia, F. (2019). Analysing the acceptation of online games in mobile devices: An application of UTAUT2. Journal of Retailing and Consumer Services, 50, 85-93.

Saha, S. (2021). Consumption pattern of OTT platforms in India. International Journal of Modern Agriculture, 10(2), 641-655.

Soares, C. (2018). The Philosophy of Individualism: A Critical Perspective. International Journal of Philosophy and Social Values. 1. 10.34632/ philosophyandsocialvalues.2018.2664.

Tamilmani, K., Rana, N.P., Dwivedi, Y.K. (2017). A Systematic Review of Citations of UTAUT2 Article and Its Usage Trends. In: , et al. Digital Nations – Smart Cities, Innovation, and Sustainability. I3E 2017. Lecture Notes in Computer Science(), vol 10595. Springer, Cham.

Wu, B., An, X., Wang, C., Shin, H.O. (2022). Extending UTAUT with national identity and fairness to understand user adoption of DCEP in China. Sci Rep 12, 6856 (2022).

THREE

ISSUES OF THE OVER-THE-TOP MEDIA COMMUNICATION AMONG TODAY'S YOUTH

Jasmine A. Assistant Professor, Holy Cross College, Department of Visual Communication, Tiruchirappalli.

Arulselvi G. Assistant Professor, Holy Cross College, Department of Visual Communication, Tiruchirappalli

Abstract

Television viewing culture is fast changing in India because of proliferation of Internet. Internet has enabled the over-the-top (OTT) media to spread rapidly in the lives of today's youth. Today, more than ever, the OTT platforms have become a more preferable choice for customers in entertainment society. The growth of the OTT market is higher due to more smartphone users. The OTT content can be delivered through the internet and smart TVs PlayStation, Chromecast, Xbox, Fire Stick and more. According to PricewaterhouseCoopers or PwC's Media and Entertainment Outlook 2020, "India's OTT market is on the way to becoming the world's sixth-largest market by 2024". Due to this massive growth watching in OTT, the growing youngsters lose their normal way of life. The culture of coming together is largely disturbed and the pattern of life has changed due to the content and innovations of OTT players. Therefore, there is a need to study the higher forums and their impact on the growing responsibilityof the youth of India.

Key Words

Over-The-Top Media, Youth, major OTT Platform, Media.

Introduction

Most of the Indian people have begun using OTT platforms as a result of the quick advancements in technology and widespread availability of the internet. The globe has literally shrunk as a result of the growth of the Internet. The global television industry has undergone a sea change as a result of the Internet.Our society is being significantly impacted by web series and streaming entertainment, especially among the young college going students The internet entertainment market in India has grown significantly during the past several years. This is made feasible by the shifting lifestyles of Indian viewers, the shift in the types of information they consume, and the variety of internet streaming services used to provide the content to them. There has been a significant increase in the number of people visiting websites for content online, as well as in the amount of time spent doing so, as a result of the introduction of faster and less expensive internet services in the form of mobile connections and widespread availability of broadband services.

Review of Literature

Dhanuka, Aditya, Bohra, Abhilash (2019)have inferred in their exploration that youth become more and more addictive towardswatching these web series. They have an adverse effect on the emotional, physical, and psychological health.**Deloitte, (2020)** in his article "Digital Media: Rise of On-demand Content" says that, "In India, thistrend is observed across diverse platforms such as audio, visual, news, music etc. Itmentions that an Indian youth, on an average spends 14% of their time and nearly17% of their monthly expenditures on entertainment. An internet content consumerin India consumes an average of 6.2 hours of content on everyday basis out ofwhich 21% of the time is spent on audio-visual entertainment". **Chatterjee and Pal (2020)**in their study discuss that the emergence of OTT has bought a huge disruption in the entire entertainment industry.There was a time when there were only two major mediums available to people for providing audio-video content which were TV and theaters. But now, with the evolution of newer technologies the scenario is changing.The OTT platforms are now changing the viewing pattern of audience and are also evolving as part of the mainstream media.

Meaning of Over the Top Media

The Abbreviation "OTT" stands for "Over-The-Top" media and refers to the productized practice of streaming content material to clients immediately over the internet. OTT is a way of providing TV and film content material over the net and to suit the necessities of the man or woman purchaser. An Over-The-top (OTT) media service is a streaming media service offered directly to viewers via the internet. OTT offerings are accessed through web sites on computer systems in addition to apps on cellular services.

The OTT represents the future of entertainment one that is already unfolding. It is also typically applied to video-on-demand platforms, but also refers to audio streaming, messaging offerings, or internet-primarily based voice calling answers. OTT offerings are generally monetized via paid subscriptions, however, there are exceptions. As an instance, some OTT platforms would possibly provide in-app purchases or advertising. OTT simply represents the destiny of media, representing the high-quality manner of leisure inside the present state of affairs. Those gaining access to OTT apps, now do so not only via subscriptions but additionally through freemium centers and the Jio effect at the streaming subculture. People additionally decide on watching regional suggests but when it comes to young adults, they prefer overseas that indicates more in comparison to the local suggests.

Objectives of Study

- To analyze viewer's perception towards OTT platform.
- To analyze the effect of using OTT platform.
- To analyze the impact of web series and streaming content on the academic performance of the hostel inmatesof college going students.

Study Methodology

The study is descriptive and empirical in nature. The sample size taken is that of 75 respondents residing in Holy Cross College Hostel, Trichy. The collection of data was done through Google forms which contains 13 relevant questions. the collection of questions was created after athorough investigation of the topic, and the set of questions intends to provide us with insights aboutthe Impactof the OTT Platform on the viewing experience of the hostel students.

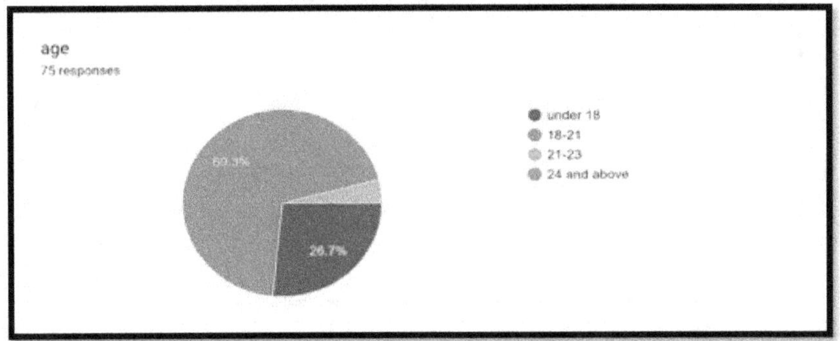

Age (figure -1)

It is clear from the above descriptive figure that the majority of the respondents underthe age 18-21are 69.3%. Whereas 26.7% of the respondents are under age of 18. Only 4% of them were between age 21-23.

(Figure -2)

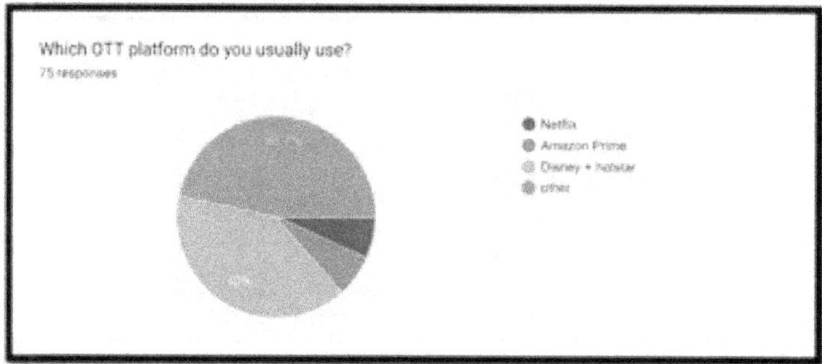

The respondents were asked about their popular online platform for streaming video content, where 46.7% prefer Instagram as their favorite online platform. 40% of the respondents chose Disney + Hot Star, while 6.7% choose Amazon, and another 6.7% choose Netflix. This clearly shows that the majority is interested in Disney + Hot Star and other channels like free video streaming on YouTube.

The reason for this is that, the majority of the students only prefer free video streaming on YouTube rather than paying subscription fee for other OTT platforms.

(Figure -3)

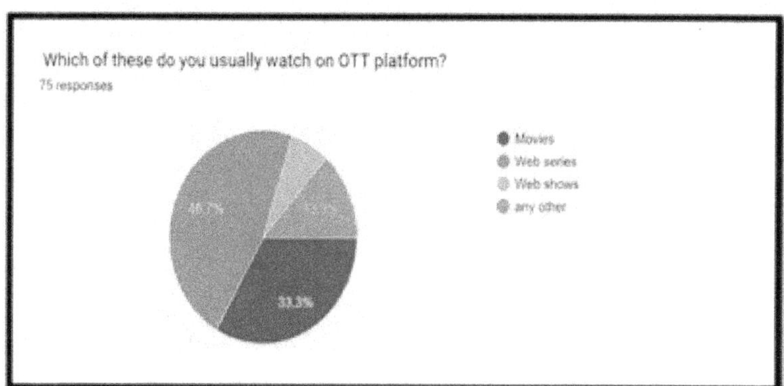

When asked the respondents about the what they usually watch on OTT,we found that the majority of the respondents about 46.7% were watching web series, 33.3% of the students were interested in watching movies, 13.3% of the students preferred to be engaged in Instagram and Facebook, while only 6.7% of them were interested in the web shows.

(Figure -4)

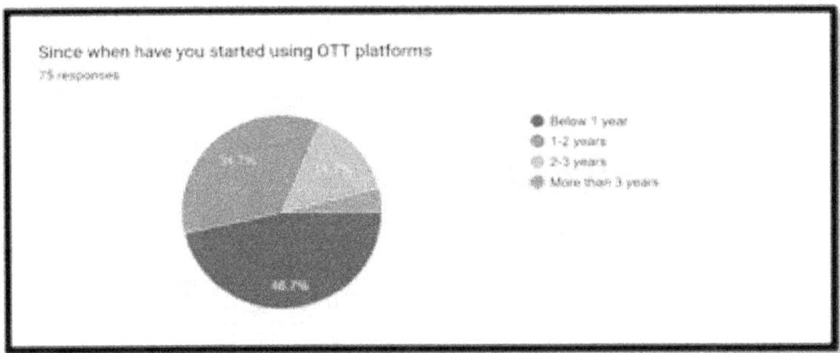

The increased preference and dependence for the OTT emerged after the pandemic covid -19. The usage of these digital platforms according to the respondents show that those who were using the OTT for about a year were 46.7% and those who have been using it for 1 or 2 years amounted to 34.7%. Only 14.7% have been using it for more than two years and only 3% of them were using it for more than 3 years. The table shows that the majority of the users have begun using the OTT just after the onset of the pandemic.

(Figure -5)

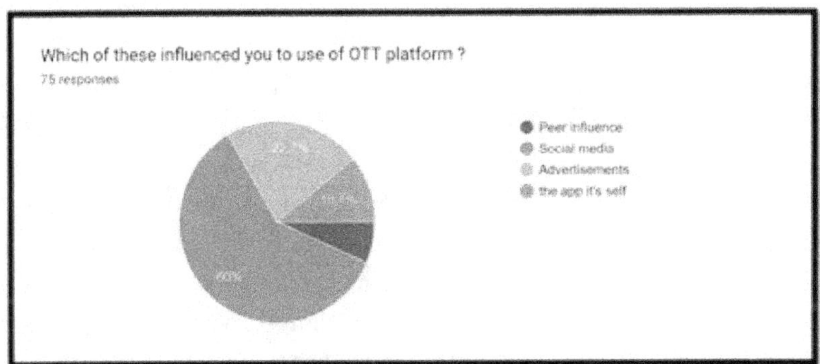

The above question aims to understand the source of information of their current OTT services. The question aims to understand which source has the highest influence on the users with regard to OTT platforms. As can be inferred, social recommendations followed by advertisements is what gets the message across the consumers of OTT platforms.

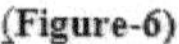

(Figure-6)

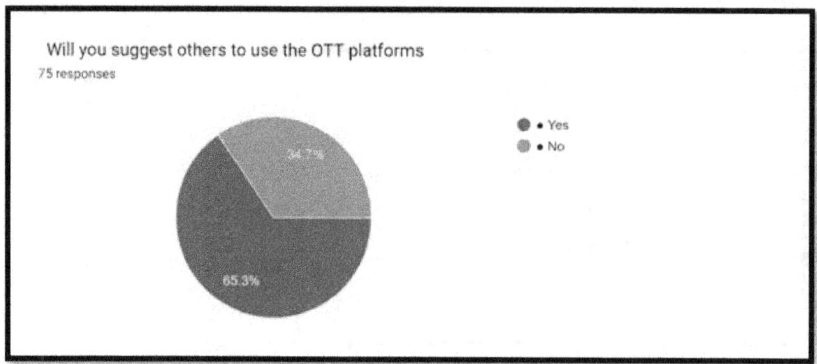

Most of the OTT services run on a business model, which involves a free trial period, after which, the customers are given a choice whether they wish to continue to use the service and subscribe to it by paying a fixed monthly fee which will give them the uninterrupted access to unlimited content provided by that streaming platform. The customers are also at a liberty to cancel the subscription anytime. Also, as satisfaction itself would not ensure repeat purchase **(Appelbaum, 2001),** it becomes imperative for the providers of OTT platforms to continuously improve technology, quality of services and the content offered on their platforms as a means to retain existing customers as well as to attract new ones.

Here in this study we find that the users themselves about 65.3% become the transmitters of the particular application to the new ones. And therefore, the majority of the users, not only that they get the benefit but also the marketing behaviour that forces them to introduce the app to others.

(Figure -7)

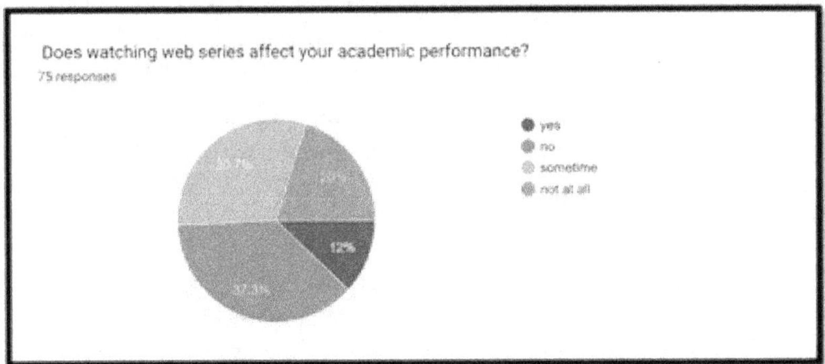

The next question was to assess whether the OTT content have affected the academic performance of the youth. Here, 12 % of the respondents agreed that watching online video streaming and web series have affected their performance in exams or other important works. 30.7% of the respondents felt that sometime it affects them. However, 57.3% disagreed to the impact of online video streaming in their academic performances.

(Figure -8)

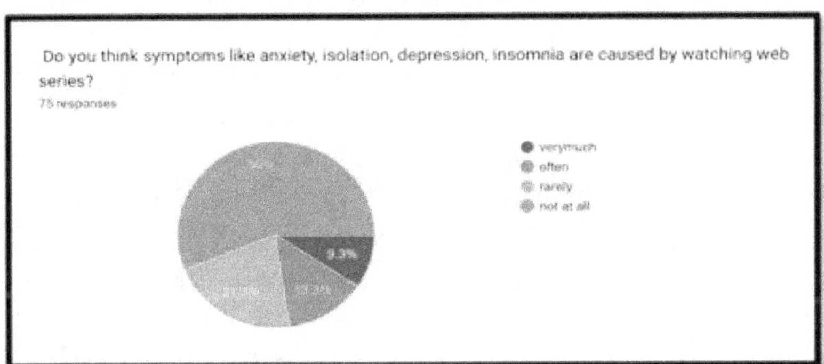

This question was formulated in order to test, whether,watching web series caused anxiety and depression amongst the students. The majority of the respondents about 56% agreed with answering 'a not at all'. While 21.3%, 13.3% and 9.3% of the respondents agreed strongly, often and rarely to that.

Therefore, the researchers' consideration falls on the 34% of the students who are affected with anxiety and depression by watching heavily on the OTT platforms.

Conclusion

We can see hundreds of web series, episodes, and videos available on OTT platforms, and several being uploaded every minute. Since they are available on the internet, it is easily accessible to the youth via smartphones or laptops. The content served here is primarily unregulated with many factors that boost the number of young college-going youth.Therefore, result clearly states that the web series and the online streaming content significantly impact the college going students both academically and psychologically.

Bibliography

1. Appelbaum, A. (2001). *The constant customer. Gallup Group.* https://news.gallup.com/businessjournal/745/ constant-customer.aspx.

2. Chatterjee, M., & Pal, S. (2020). *Globalization propelled technology often ends up in its microlocalization: Cinema viewing in the time of OTT.* Global Media Journal: Indian Edition, 12(1).

3. Deloitte. *Digital Media: Rise of On-demand Content.* Retrieved April 15, 2020,from **https://www2.deloitte.com/content/dam/Deloitte/in/ Documents/technology-mediatelecommunications/in-tmt-rise-of-on-demand-content.pdf**.

4. Dhiman B (2021) *The Practice of Media Education and Media Research: A Review on Five Asian Countries.* Global Media Journal, 19:1-7.

5. Singh, D. 2020, *"How is coronavirus impacting the streaming platforms with an increasing appetite of viewers".* Retrieved from Financial express: **https://www.financialexpress.com/brandwagon/how-is-coronavirus-impacting-the- streamingplatforms-with-an-increasing-appetite-of-viewers/1919916**.

6. Varghese, S., &Chinnaiah, S. (2021). *IS OTT INDUSTRY A DISRUPTION TO MOVIE THEATRE INDUSTRY?* Academy of Marketing Studies Journal, 25(2), 1-12.

FOUR

REGIONAL OTT PLATFORMS: A SHIFT FROM GLOBAL TO LOCAL

Shruti Shukla[1] and Dr. Junali Deka[2]

Research Scholar[1], Department of Mass Communication & Journalism, Tezpur University, Assam, (email: shrutishukla2612@gmail.com)

Assistant Professor[2], Department of Mass Communication & Journalism, Tezpur University, Assam, (email: junalid@tezu.ernet.in)

Abstract

In the Over theTop (OTT) era, personalised entertainment has grown up in compared to broadcasting media, one way of personalising is providing content in regional language. With most of the big OTT platforms focussing primarily on Hindi and English content, a new set of OTT platforms are emerging in the regional markets that cater to local issues and concerns. While the big and established OTT playersare targeting a global and diverse audience population, the regional OTT players are mainlyaiming to meet the content needs of native viewers. The year 2021 has seen growth of the regional OTT platforms in the states of Maharashtra, Gujarat, Kerala, Karnataka, Andhra Pradesh, Telangana and Tamil Nadu. Some of the well-known platforms are *Aha* (Telugu), *Hoichoi* (Bengali), *Planet Marathi*, *Koode* (Malayalam), and *City Short TV* (Gujarati), etc. According to a FICCI-PwC report2021 (Federation of Indian Chambers of Commerce and

Industry-PriceWaterHouseCoopers), the share of regional language consumption on OTT platforms to cross 50% of total time spent by 2025, easing past Hindi at 45%. This paper is an attempt to find out the emergence, advantage, challenges of regional streaming services in India through exploratory research.The findings revealed that 'region centric content', 'personalized experience', and 'technological flexibility' are significant reasons for the increasing popularity of regional OTT platforms. The regional OTT platforms are gaining more acceptance and popularity with their generic content in the country.

Keywords: OTT, Regional Media, Entertainment

Introduction

Through online streaming or Video on Demand (VoD) services, recent technological improvements have made watching movies or TV shows more convenient. OTT or "Over-the-top" means video content streamed through internet and not through broadcast or cable television. Any Internet-connected device, including a smartphone, smart TV, tablet, desktop computer, laptop, etc., can be used by viewers to access video content via OTT apps. With Netflix starting its service in India in January 2016, followed by Voot from Viacom18, and Amazon's Prime Video ultimately arriving in December 2016, both international and domestic OTT businesses quickly joined the market. In October 2016, Reliance Jio started, gaining access to free high-speed 4G internet for over 70 million mobile customers (*The Economic Times*, 02 Mar, 2017). This allowed OTT players to flourish while also assisting the businesses in growing their subscription bases and user engagement. The most important components continue to be appealing content and a seamless user experience.

With a population of over 130 billion people, 60% of whom are under 25, and only a few entertainment options available, India is a particularly alluring market for both content producers and distributors. For the millions of viewers searching for change and control, the availability of numerous digital content distribution platforms with high-quality, original content and the freedom to watch anywhere, anytime, is a great alternative.According to a survey by the Boston Consulting Group (BCG) and the CII(Confederation of Indian Industry), India's average digital video consumption increased two times in the previous two years. The research also noted that Indians' daily average time spent watching videos climbed from 11 to 24 minutes (as of November 2019).According to the PwC, Global Entertainment & Media outlook: 2020–2024 research, the proliferation of

Smartphone devices and internet-connected television sets has led to an increase in OTT video content consumption both inside and outside the home. The main source of revenue will be subscription VOD, which is expected to grow at a 30.7 percent CAGR (Compound Annual Growth Rate) from US$708 million in 2019 to US$2.7 billion in 2024.According to the report, India's OTT industry is expanding at the fastest rate, with a 28.6 percent CAGR, and is expected to rank sixth in size by 2024. In 2024, the OTT market in India will surpass those in South Korea, Germany, and Australia to take the sixth-largest position.

According to SBI Research (2022),'The OTT industry is anticipated to expand from Rs 2,590 crore in 2018 to Rs 11,944 crore by 2023, representing the CAGR of 36 %. With over 40 players and original media content available in all languages, OTT has already taken 7-9% of the revenue and market share of the entertainment sector'. The OTT channels expanded the audience for regional content, which previously had a little following. Now, people can readily access the television programmes and films produced in regional industries in Marathi, Gujarati, Malayalam, Assamese, Odia, Telugu, and many more languages.OTT platforms are just getting started, while traditional content producers and distribution channels are slowly dying.It has been noted that 70% of Gujarati speakers prefer content in their mother tongue, compared to 69% of Telugu speakers, 90% of Tamil speakers, 64% of Marathi speakers, 91% of Kannada speakers, and 77% of Bengali speakers(Waghmare, G.2022).This demonstrates the growing desire for native-language content. The opportunities and difficulties in the development of regional OTT platforms will be examined in the current research.

Literature Review

Ganesh Waghmare et.al (2022)in their article *'Growth of Over-The-Top (OTT) video services in India'*studied the factors which influence sudden growth of OTT player in India. The research is based on secondary data analysis. The findings reveals that the ease of mobility that these OTT platforms offer is a major component in the expansion of OTT platforms. The consumer is willing to pay more money as long as they have the freedom and flexibility to watch whatever they want, wherever they are. It is anticipated by the researcher that countries like China and India would see a rapid increase in the number of people using pay-per-view and video streaming services. The primary elements encouraging the expansion of OTT platforms in India include comfort, mobility, COVID-19 lockdown, high-quality content on the platforms, and the availability of content in regional languages.

Kaneenika Jain (2021) *'The rise of OTT platforms:Changing consumer preferences'* highlights the rise of OTT, causes contributing to its success, and the key players serving the target demographic. The research is based on secondary data. A key finding shows that the pandemic Covid 19 has significantly influenced the subscription of popular OTT services because of the abundance of free time and demand for entertainment and edutainment during lockdown. According to trends, the OTT market will expand quickly over the next few years as well.

Veer P Gangwar et.al (2020) *'Profiles and Preferences of OTT users in Indian Perspective'*, the article takes a look at OTT user profiles and preferences from an Indian viewpoint.The study makes use of the questionnaire method, for selecting samples non-probability sampling is employed. The "Innovation Adoption Model" and "User and Gratification Theory" are the theoretical frameworks employed in the study.According to the current study, user profiles and content choices vary. Although there has been significant investment in OTT platforms, it is still difficult to predict that they will displace current TV systems.The millennium is drawn to OTT services because they offer video on demand and foreign content. The emergence of JIO and its provision of 4G services at no cost significantly aids OTT platforms in their rapid growth.

Research Objectives

1. To find out the emerging OTT platforms in regional languages in India.
2. To study the opportunities and challenges for regional OTT market.

Findings and Discussion

The research article presents an insight to the growing OTT platforms in local language apart from the dominant languages such as Hindi and English. The available OTT services deliver content primarily in Hindi which has failed to be representative in dealing with issues, topics which are regioncentric.It is clear that usage and popularity of OTT platforms have only increased since their introduction. Covid 19 Lockdown has resulted in an exponential rise in popularity and an abrupt change in how people consume entertainment across many media channels. People were found to use OTT platforms more frequently than conventional platforms, including television, for entertainment and information.

Rise of regional OTT players in India

With the help of secondary data, the study found that there are currently about 46 providers of over-the-top media services in India, which distribute streaming media over the Internet. A few popular regional OTT channels of recent times are Hoichoi (2017)- Bengali OTT channel, Aha (2020)-Telugu and Tamil content, Sun NXT (2017)- offers content in Tamil, Telugu, Malayalam, Kannada, Bengali and Marathi, Koode (2020)- first independent OTT platform to offer Malayalam content, Addatimes (2016) caters to the Bengali viewers, Planet Marathi (2020)- in Marathi, Olly Plus (2020)- in Odia, OHO Gujarati (2021)- in Gujarati, Talkies (2020) -in Konkani, Tulu, Kannada, Reel Drama (2021)- for Assamese content (*The Indian Express*, 2021)

Opportunities for Regional OTT players

According to a latest analysis by MPA (Media Partner Aisa,2022), India's streaming video business is in its second development phase, with revenues of $3 billion in 2022 anticipated to more than double to approximately $7 billion by 2027. According to MPA data, India had 97 million OTT subscribers by the end of March 2022 (Mint, July 2022).The industry is predicted to develop as a result of rising internet usage, the Bring Your Own Device (BYOD) trend, rising cloud computing adoption, and falling smartphone and data pack pricing. In India, new local players are gearing to grab the market share.According to a latest FICCI EY report (2022), the share of regional languages in all OTT video content will double from 27% in 2020 to 54% in 2024 as more streaming platforms embrace vernacular programmes and films.Currently, in India there are 1.18 billion mobile connections, 700 million Internet users, and 600 million smartphones, with a per quarter growth rate of 25 million, has the highest data consumption which is about 12 GB per person a month with better connectivity. (*The Economic Times*, 2021). There is room for regional OTT channels to expand, as seen by the rise in demand for smartphones, growing use of mobile data, demand of regional language content and an increase in the number of online video viewers in India.

Challenges for Regional language OTT Channels

For regional over-the-top (OTT) video platforms competing for viewers with well-funded international firms like Netflix, Amazon Prime Video, and Disney+Hotstar, the streaming business is becoming more and more expensive.Due to the high fees for actors, directors, and writers, smaller OTT platforms find it challenging to grow, but large OTT channels find it simple to raise capital. Local channels struggle to produce original web series.The senior management official of Hoichoi discussed about the challenges in running regional OTT services in an interview with *'The Mint'* (2022). Soumya Mukherjee, chief operating officer of Hoichoi said, *'Justifying every piece of content on the platform is a problem for us because production expenses are increasing. As a result, we are quite selective about what we approve. We refrain from it until we believe it has the X-factor or the necessary strength to offer audiences high-quality entertainment.'*

Conclusion

Indian being a diverse country in terms of culture, language and identity, one language content fails to connect to the issues of people and region of different part of the nation.With the rising demand from audience to cater to the needs of their likes and interests, media too is shaping content to satisfy this diverse group of entertainment viewers. Similarly, OTT platforms are also shifting from global content to the local content and it has been accepted in various languages namely Bengali, Marathi, Odia, Kannada, Tamil, Telugu, Assameseetc. With the entertainment content, there is also visible intervention of regional language advertisements online platforms. It has been understood that the established and known OTT players such as Netflix and Amazon Prime have subscribers for mostly content in Hindi and English.

It can be concluded that the demand for regional content will increase in the coming years and surely led to the demassification of the Indian audience.

Reference

Jain, K. (2021, June). The rise of OTT platform: Changing consumer preferences. *EPRA International Journal of Multidisciplinary Research (IJMR)*, 7(6). https://eprajournals.com/IJMR/article/5241/abstract

Waghmare, G. et, al. (2022, February). Growth of over-the-top (OTT) video services in India. *The British Journal of Administrative Management*, 58(147). https://www.researchgate.net/publication/360889303_GROWTH_OFOVER-THE-TOP_OTT_VIDEOSERVICES_IN_INDIA

Team, W. B. S. (2022, July 25). Indias OTT market likely to touch $7 billion by 2027, says report. *www.Business-Standard.Com*. Retrieved September 29, 2022, from https://www.business-standard.com/article/companies/india-s-ott-market-likely-to-touch-7-billion-by-2027-says-report-122072501324_1.html

Online, E. T. (2022, August 26). OTT about to dethrone multiplexes as India's go-to entertainment option. *The Economic Times*. Retrieved

September 29, 2022, from https://economictimes.indiatimes.com/industry/media/entertainment/ott-about-to-dethrone-multiplexes-as-indias-go-to-entertainment-option/articleshow/93804480.cms?from=mdr

Jha, L. (2022, August 2). Local OTT platforms battle rising costs of production | Mint. *Mint.* Retrieved September 29, 2022, from https://www.livemint.com/industry/media/local-ott-platforms-battle-rising-costs-of-production-11659381966885.html

Moniz, C. (2022, June 28). Regional OTT content: Spreading the net. *Financial Express.* Retrieved September 29, 2022, from https://www.financialexpress.com/brandwagon/regional-ott-content-spreading-the-net/2573672/

How regional language content is impacting OTT. (2022, June 12). *Financial Express.* Retrieved September 29, 2022, from https://www.financialexpress.com/brandwagon/how-regional-language-content-is-impacting-ott/2557586/

Abbas, M. (2021, October 26). India's growing data usage, smartphone adoption to boost Digital India initiatives: Top bureaucrat. *The Economic Times.* Retrieved September 29, 2022, from https://economictimes.indiatimes.com/news/india/indias-growing-data-usage-smartphone-adoption-to-boost-digital-india-initiatives-top-bureaucrat/articleshow/87275402.cms?from=mdr

Jain, A. (2021, June 1). Beyond Netflix, Hotstar, and Prime Video: 13 regional OTT platforms for your daily entertainment fix. *The Indian Express.* Retrieved September 30, 2022, from https://indianexpress.com/article/entertainment/web-series/13-ott-platforms-that-offer-content-in-several-regional-languages-7335566/

FIVE

Portrayal of Women in Cable TV and OTT Hindi series

Ameena Kulsum Khan

PhD Scholar, Karnataka State Open University, Mysore

Dr Hemalatha R

Assistant Professor

DOSR in Journalism and mass communication

Abstract:

OTT (Over the top) platforms has altered the way Indians consume entertainment. This platform hassomething for everyone, be it young or an old person. The technological advancement has enabled the audience to consume content anytime anywhere. Contrary to traditional media, OTT platforms present a variety of tales without censorship, box office, or audience restrictions.

Here the audience have the liberty to view local as well as global shows. The localisation of content has helped shows reach to a much larger audience. It would not be wrong to say that over the years, OTT platform has carved its place in the market.

This platform has also opened the opportunitiesfor the new content creators to tell their stories. It has helped bring newness in the format and narrative of the stories that were being told on the traditional media.

One such topic of interest has been the way women are portrayed on screen.The goal of this paper is to understand howwomen are portrayed in web series. How similar or different are the portrayal of Women compared to the traditional media platforms. And how the global & regional OTT platforms have contributed to making this change in the narratives of the web series over time.

Key Words: Web series, TV serials, gender roles, localisation, globalization &glocalization.

Introduction:

In the 1930, televisions serials/ soup operas started off as a representation of massively popular gerne of pause serial home radio dramas. Today they have become an essential part of many households across the globe. According to the Advertising & Media Outlook, there are at least 5.36 billion TV viewers around the world.

TV serials in India can be dated back to the 1980's when India's first ever television drama 'Hum Log' was aired with 154 episodes. In the early 90s, millions of Indian families tuned in to watch Mythological dramas like *Ramayana &Mahabharata*.It went on to become the longestTV serial in Indian Television history. Ever since serials have become an integral part of the people's life.Mass media has in many ways helped shape the social realities through its content (Fareed Ahmad, 2014, p.1)

The privatization of channels opened the opportunities for the advent of international channels in India. It led to the introduction ofthe 24x7 programme format, new technology in production and helped the audience learn about new religion as well as the culture from across the globe.

The serials being produced during this period were a combination of biographies, crime drama & daytime dramas. This enables TV channels to reach viewers beyond their target audience.

OTT platforms

The advancement of technology led to the emergence of (over-the-top) OTT platforms. This is an online streaming platform. According to an article by McAdams, M.'s (2021) What Is OTT? – Understanding The Modern Media Streaming Landscape (Tapjoy) he says that OTT platform also refers to internet-based direct messaging services, audio, podcast streaming, and video services.

This has changed the viewing experience of the audience by giving them the option of enjoying the content at the comfort of their homes. These services are paid through subscription basis. As stated by Sundaravel and Elangovan (2020), one of the primary reasons for the success and growth of OTT platforms is its pricing and the convenience of getting personalised content.

The way content is produced and distributed has also seen a drastic change due to the OTT platforms. The use of Artificial intelligence in such apps recommends the audience content based on their previous viewing history. On OTT platforms the users get to choose from a variety of national & international shows.

The growing demand of OTT content has led to the expansion of the market for such platforms. In a recent study by Frost & Sullivan's (2018) found that, the Indian OTT video market has started to gain traction with more rivals and new creative platforms thanks to more affordable data bundles. Today the Indian market has a combination of both national and international players like Amazon, Netflix, Voot, ALT Balaji and many more.

Different techniques such as subtitles and dubbing of international content into local languages has helped the content on OTT platforms reach a larger audience in India.

Today most of the platformsgive the choice to the audience to view content in their desired local languages. This to a large extent has blurred the lines between global and regional content. In an article by Niharika Lal *'The Indian audience's growing appetite for global OTT content'*ApekshaVakharia, Marketing Director, Asia-Pacific Content, MUBI, said that over the years, Indian audiences have demonstrated a strong appetite for global cinema and since the pandemic, this only continued to grow. There is now an even wider hunger for rich stories, cutting across languages and genres.

The exposure to global content has helped the audience learn about different cultures and counties which otherwise seemed impossible. Few such examples are the popularity and success of Korean & Spanish shows in India.

Women in Hindi serials

Advent of satellite television altered how people perceived the world. The media is crucial in shaping and directing new identities in society. This has implications on gender, both domestically and internationally (Datta,2000).

The dominant gender roles in society have a large influence on Indian serials. Gender stereotypes are generalised beliefs about the characteristics and qualities that society attributes to men and women (Eagly, 1987). In most cases, the portrayal of a woman in serials is done to appease societal social norms.

We have observed that most of the TV serials featuring women portray them as physically feeble, submissive, involved in housework, and the only thing they do is provide care to their families. They are also portrayed as miserable, mindless, and self-sacrificing creatures (Desai, 1996). The male, on the other hand, is a physically powerful, dominating individual who provides for the family's needs.

The female characters in most serials wear traditional outfits, designer sarees, and gold jewellery. This demonstrates a patriarchal society in which the woman dressed traditionally is respected in society. The audience expects the heroines to show their devotion to tradition by dressing in Indian attire (Josiam.B.,M& Strubel.J,2016, pg: 317).

In the majority of Hindi television series, women are primarily depicted working in the kitchen or performing housework. In most cases it is observed that serials' stories revolve around women from upper-class and wealthy families. As a result, they are always seen wearing designer sarees and gold jewellery. It can be seen that regardless of how educated the woman is, she is considered to be a 'good' woman if she is confined within the house. Making certain she looks after her husband, family, and in-laws. While the nature of the man's role is dominating. He is regarded as the family breadwinner and makes all domestic decisions. He is portrayed as strong, successful, and wealthy.

In serials like*Saath Nibhana Saathiya (2010), Yeh Rista Kya Khelatha Hai (2009), Baade Ache Lagte Hai (2011)* we can see that the women are well groomed all the time. But they are never shown in an intelligent, confident roles. They are also expected to obey or abide by the decisions made by the man or her family without questioning. Women in these serials are not expected to raise their voice or question the injustice.

Women's roles are oversimplified, resulting in women playing either the protagonist or the vamp (Ross. L, 2009). In most cases, the outspoken and confident woman is dressed in western attire and is portrayed as a vamp. While the soft-spoken and submissive woman is the protagonist. This leaves no room for portraying women as they truly are.

A woman's bold and independent character is portrayed negatively. Their struggles have authenticated because they have chosen to stand up for themselves. She is also regarded as a woman of questionable character. A widow or divorcee is typically cast in the role of a non-traditional woman.

The characterisation of women is further broken down into traditional and non-traditional. The traditional women are the ones who abide by the rules stays at home and takes care of the family. On the other hand, the non-traditional woman are the ones who desire to be economically independent (Kataria.M&Pandey.B 2014).

However, in recent years, there have been significant changes in the way women are portrayed in Hindi serials.

Women are increasingly taking centre stage in serials in recent years. They are shown working and providing for their families. However, they are expected to care for their children and families after work in order to pursue their careers. The female roles must balance family and work. Women are expected to be superhumans who manage both the home and the job, according to Pandey, M. (1991). Women's accomplishments are measured by how well they handle household responsibilities. Over her professional talent and success.

In a few serials, we observe that other characters take control of the woman's life in the absence of a dominating male character. For instance, the lead character Gopi's spouse in *SaathNibhaana Saathiya (2010)* does not frequently meddle in her and the family's affairs. However, Gopi's mother-in-law Kokila Bhen is always dictating choices for her. According to *Charkarborty. G (2015)*, when a dominant man is replaced with a woman, the woman is portrayed as a symbolic male. She continues by saying that the dominant character can be played by either a mother, sister-in-law, or mother.

The introduction of original content on online streaming platforms (OTT platforms) has provided the entertainment industry with a fantastic opportunity to experiment with various content types. According to Sana Farzeen's article from 2019 titled "OTT platforms a boon for women-centric content," the paradigm shift in the type of content on OTT platforms is not simply about having a cast that is led by women. Additionally, it concerns female-driven content that is no longer centred on family drama or the typical saas-bahu repertory.

This has resulted in an increase in the popularity of women-centric serials on OTT platforms. Because of her, women have begun to take centre stage. There have been numerous examples of female-led serials, such as Arya (2021), Lust stories (2018), Geelipuchi (2021), and other international shows.

It wouldn't be wrong to say that the audience's exposure to international content on OTT platforms may have an impact on the need for freshness in locally available content. Because of this, serials may have been compelled to abandon the conventional wisdom that a male must play the lead part in order for a serial to succeed. But it's still clear that the women in the series are portrayed as being dependent on a guy or other strong character to lead them or make decisions for them.

According to Raval D.M. (2020), viewers have access to powerful content to explore online and on digital platforms thanks to web series produced all over the world. More female-centric stories are now possible thanks to the web series on OTT platforms. Ruchi Narain claimed in an article titled Female's the way on OTT: Women-fronted stories rule the web by Shreya Mukherjee (2020) that OTT platforms must meet audience preferences by providing narratives they can relate to and mimic, as it is a current market demand. Women are sick and weary of being presented as giving and altruistic. Additionally, they want to be allowed to pursue their goals, have fun, and have life-changing experiences—all traits that, until recently, were reserved for men only.

Conclusion:

Over time the content and platforms available to the audience has evolved. This could be due to many reasons such as advancement of technology, exposure to global contentand vast options of entertainment.

This has not just changed the viewing experience of the audience but also has influenced the type of content that they consume. OTT platforms has largely blurred the lines between the local and global content. The effort of international OTT platforms like Amazon prime and Netflix to provide glocalisedcontent has help them reach larger audience. This technique has opened up new opportunities for expansion of the content and the platforms to reach newer audience which otherwise was not possible.

OTT platform helped in the evolution of the was content is consumed as well as produced. It has not just introduced the world to different format of content but also different technique of content creation. Based on the observations made, it can be said that the content on OTT platform has contributedin the evolution of the narrative around women. It could also be said that the exposure to vast global content could have influenced the audience's demandfor newness in the content that is locally available.

References:

1. Abramson. A (2007)The History of Television, 1942 to 2000 McFarland, Incorporated, Publishers, Pages 1-308.

2. Desai, P (1996) An analytical study of the portrayal of women in Indian soap operas

3. Dutta.S (2002) Globalization and representation of women in Indian Cinema, Social Scientist, Vol.28

4. Dhar S ;Pattnaik S.N. (1996) 'Portrayal of Distorted image of Women by Indian Media',Communicator, Vol-31,

5. Eagly,A.H., Steffen ,V.J.,(1984) Gender stereotypes stem from the distribution of women and men into social roles. Journal of personality and social psychology, Vol. 46(4), Pg. 735-754

6. Gudipaty. N (2018) Representation of 'family' in Indian television serials

7. HimashreePatowary (2014) Portrayal of Women in Indian Mass Media: An Investigation,Vol. 1 No. 1

8. Madhusmita Das, Sangeeta Sharma. (2021) Should I be portrayed like this? An exploration of Indian women in television advertising. Feminist Media Studies 0:0, pages 1-18.

9. Roy.D (2012) REALITY OR MYTH: REPRESENTATION OF WOMEN IN INDIAN TV SERIALS. Global Media Journal, Vol. 3/No.

10. McAdams, M. (2021). What Is OTT? – Understanding The Modern Media Streaming Landscape – tapjoy.com. Norman. k, & Y.vonna (1998) Qualitative Research Methods for Media Studies

11. Nijhawan.G.S, & Dahiya.S, 2020, Role of Covid as a catalyst in increasing adoption ofOTTs in India: A study of evolving consumer consumption patterns and future business scope

12. Pal BK (1987) ` Problems and concerns of Indian women' ABC Publishing House 72

13. Pandey, M. (1991). The Subject is Women, New Delhi, Sanchar Publishing House

14. Ray. A (2014) A study on the Soap Operas in Indian Private TV channels

15. Raval D.M (2020) A Study on Impact & Popularity of Web Series on Youth Vol 8, Issue 9

16. Ross. L, (2009) from the 'F' word to indigenous/feminism, University of Minnesota press Vol.24, Pg:39-52

17. Sant.S (2020) A study on factors leading to adoption of OTT services among millennial consumers in India, Vol 1 issue 2

18. Singhal.A& Rogers.E., V (1988) Television soap operas for development in India

19. Shreya Mukherjee (2020) Female's the way on OTT: Women-fronted stories rule the web

20. Sundaravel. E & Elangovan N. (2020) Emergence and future of Over-the-top (OTT) video services in India: An analytical research

21. Shanker Market, New Delhi-1 pp 91-94.

22. Syed A.H., B (2011) What is Comparative Study

23. Sodhi, U., & Roy, N. (2021). Evolution in OTT space in India: Where next wave of growth will come from

24. Sundaravel, E. & N., Elangovan. (2020). Emergence and future of Over-the-top (OTT) video services in India: an analytical research. International Journal of Business Management and Social Research. 8. 489-499.

25. Patowary. H (2014) Portrayal of Women in Indian Mass Media: An Investigation, Journal of Education & Social Policy, Vol. 1 No. 1

26. Srirupa Chatterjee, Shreya Rastogi. (2022) Television culture and the beauty bias problem: an analysis of India's postmillennial television serials. Media Asia 49:3, pages 213-234.

SIX

A SOCIO-CULTURAL & POLITICAL CRITICISM TO COMPARATIVE STUDY ON "IMSAI ARASAN 23RD PULICACI" (TORTURE KING 23RD PULICACI) AND "MANDELA"

Broskhan. P[1] Dr. Nelsonmandela.S[2]

[1]*Research Scholar, Department of Visual Communication, Faculty of Science and Humanities, SRM Institute of Science and Technology, Tamilnadu*
bp4756@srmist.edu.in

[2]*Assistant Professor, Department of Visual Communication, Faculty of Science and Humanities, SRM Institute of Science and Technology, Tamilnadu*
nelsonms@srmist.edu.in

Abstract

Film has long been a part of the entertainment industry. It has a huge impact on people all over the world. However, cinema is a very strong cultural practice and system. Comedy is now considered important. Humor is based on works that contain ideas and critiques of social and political issues. The purpose of this study is to transform comedy films into tools and agents of social criticism. Therefore, the purpose of this study is to transform the criticism of comedy films into a critical medium. Tamil films include polemics and criticisms on socio-cultural, traditional and political issues. And it will be featured in periodical movies. The structure of comedy is important as a critique of socio-culture, and it manifests itself intensely. Similarly, to know the ratio of opinions between two major comedy films released in a certain time period and the socio-political position in the contemporary situation, the films *"ImsaiArasan 23AM Pulikesi"* released in 2006 and *"Mandela"* released in 2021 indicate two different time situations. The aim of this study is to do a comparative analysis of the above mentioned two films which can play an important role as social and political criticism.

Keywords: Tamil Cinema, Criticism, Comedy, Entertainment,Cultural

Introduction

Humor is a creative idea that is created to make the audience laugh or stimulate their sense of humor(King, 2002). The comedy film creates laughter through the interpretation of the caricature character and comedy scenes.Humor is a serious genre.The comic reflects various thoughts, social activities and political critiques(Bishop, 2014).

There are numerous types of comedic film. There will be film comedy as long as the movie is an entertainment medium. Humor was one of the most popular forms of comedy in cinema in the early days, and the development of comedies has been rampant ever since. A reference in the film 'The Water Watered' released in 1895(Lumière, 1895).

Various studies have been instrumental in the discussion of the potential elements of cultural and political critique of cinema and comedy. Thus, film comedy involves dialogue in two main and interrelated ways(Cherry, 2021). First, he argues that comedy should be emphasized or centered in films as a means of performing political and cultural critiques. Second, it focuses more on the cultural and political formation that has evolved from the very basis of cinema.(Robert L. Hardgrave)

Tami film comedy can be used as a thesis in identifying caste, ethnicity, politics and high culture through film story representation. Many cultural studies have suggested that by focusing on the cultural and traditional forms experienced by the majority of the population, it allows us to understand how 'common sense' develops and its effect, helping ordinary people to manage in unknown ways. Too many people are too far away from their own interests'. (Susairaj, 2020)

Political Satire

As Cesare said, it is 'intrinsic discovery'. Educating people does not mean politics, politics does not mean talking. Its meaning is to teach people that everything depends on them to try relentlessly and enthusiastically. Friends Fanon, The Reach of the Earth (Wayne, Political film, 2001) satire has long been a tool of political criticism. Political satire video and diversified memes will only inform the public of the seriousness of a particular problem and will not provide a solution. It is not their job to find a solution to those social problems and to find a solution to them; political satire is a kind of satire.

Political satire is generally completely different from other satires. Political opposition or political dissent does not necessarily carry an agenda or seek to influence the political process. During Hitler's rule, the mockery of the political system and its holes was made clear by the filmmaker Charlie Chaplin (The Great Dictator). Political satire movies may only seem humorous in some ways but it also points our way Political systems point to a strong resistance against its nature in the current context (Selvan, 2017).

ImsaiArasan 23rd Pulicaci(Simbudevan, 2006) is a film set in India during the British rule. An imaginary area called "Cholapurapalayam" is the place where the screen was created to appear under the British rule. The film describes the reign of a short-lived monarch whose people are affected by his actions in the region. Caste conflicts during the reign of King *(Actor Vadivelu)* and the emergence of foreign soft drinks have left important loopholes in the current political system. And King Pulicaci is the king who supported the British. "Simbudevan" has chosen the Salvador Dali mustache for the most imaginative bulge. This development of the upper lip as he knew it could become an ideological symbol of Hitler or Bharati. and the character of "Ukhraputhan", who comes later in the film, would have played the role of a great reformer and revolutionary leader against the English state. This film has been selected for research intact and is considered one of the most important of its kind.

The *"Mandela"(Ashwin, 2021)* film is based on a storyline that is politicized based on caste. Actor "Yogi Babu", popularly known as "Ilichchavayan" (Smile), lives in isolation from the people of the village. Contemporary caste atrocities are exposed by showing the ins and outs of caste atrocities such as refusing permission through the front door of the house, sitting on the floor without sitting on the bus seat, and forcing people to clean the public toilet. The two sons born to the two caste wives of the elder of the village head are standing separately in the contest as to who will be the next village head. Both have equal votes, counting on two different caste votes. Yogibabu has a drive to win. So both the caste candidates are doing all the necessities for Yogibabu. That is what makes his life dangerous. Yogibabu, who was selfish for more than a point, uses that single hole tool to meet all the needs of the city and get the assumption of the people. The director has turned the political hoax for that single ballot into a political satire. Selected for research is considered one of the most important of its kind.

Problem Statement

To this extent, cultural studies offer two reasons, such as comedy films, for taking popular culture seriously. Both, the films function as a socially and politically and meaningfully 'institution'. The films suggest dialogue for the interests of the powerful who represent the political machine. The Tamil comedy film genre is often criticized in the early days and classified as substandard - because they are viewed by the print media as substandard due to their substance.

Therefore, these circumstances demonstrate the fundamental gap for this research. In this context, this research argues that Tamil comedy is greatly affected by sociocultural-political events and changes. At such a juncture, this research argues that the Tamil comedy genre is affected by socio-political events and cultural changes. Thus, it acts as a representative body that creates and exemplifies a unique national identity for all of us. In that note the focus of this research is on comedy film as an agent critical of society (Hoon Lee, 2014) . So this study is to explore the critique of comedy cinema as a critical medium. The insight of this research was built through quality research design.

The purpose of this research is to critique reviews on social organization, culture and political in the framework of humor. The purpose of the study is to analyze comedy films that are capable of playing a specific role as a critique of society. Based on some of the above tips it is possible to know that comedy film is influenced by social culture to some extent with regard to further discoveries.

Literature Review

Many films have been released in Tamil that have made a mockery of the current political and governmental flaws. It is a popular saying in the history of Tamil cinema to mock and ridicule political events of a particular period. As far as Tamil cinema is concerned these may be some of the most important films under political satire: Mohammad bin Tughlaq (1971), Peace Corps (1994), Joker (2016). ImsaiArasan 23rd Pulicaci (2010) is a fantasy film. It has ridiculed the suffering of the people by a foolish government (Selvan, 2017).

This applies to all phases. It makes fun of the current critical holes. Problems such as political turmoil, caste conflicts, foreign trade and the monarchy mess remain unresolved in any period. This research reveals through visual analysis of the satirical features handled in the film. The film uses a standard method based on Semiotics(S.R. Ravikumar, 2020). The study examines how the film contributed as a catalyst towards development, and the study says that the detail of the social issues discussed in the film has been brought through this study.

Usually dark skinned, short, plump bodies play a role as a base for violence and humor. Being teased is routine. It resonates in cinema as well. Violent and contradictory or humorous and outwardly present, the modern space has been systematized. It seeks to establish that Malayalee's in Malayalam cinema accept slightly inferior rooted humor. This study has shown that the image of comedy has changed in the Kerala tradition and there has been a somewhat perverse mindset in the metaphorical portrayals of the controversial political satire. That explains why it has affected the community as well.(Kuriakose, 2019)

Claim that indirect arguments against minorities will no longer exist in the United States. In Hollywood movies, stereotypes are often used as comedy. Over the past decade comedies such as Evan Almighty (2007), Wild Hogs (2007), Meet Dave (2008), The Maiden Heist (2009), Last Vegas (2013), Someone Marry Barry (2014) Going in Style (2017) Showed no racism on the surface. In this way it is healthy to think that humor-centric imagery is avoided and racism is changed. This research effort seeks to see how Hollywood presents racism in comedy films, especially in the last decade. Representation theory was used to interpret seven comedy films, scenes, and dialogues related to racism. Humor theory has also been used to understand how racist comedy is characterized by African-American characters. The finding of this research indicates that the negative images and stereotypes of African Americans in Hollywood movies are still enduring.(Thiska Septa Maiza, 2019)

The desire for comedy in India is on the rise. Comedy is the sequel to Stunt Comedy. People with a heavy workload, as well as depressed upper middle class people, are wandering in search of the need for humor. So stunt comedy has emerged as a stand-alone industry. But mostly the audience that participates in a show like this and the comedian who speaks on the show are upper class castes (Mintz, 1985).There is an allegation that those comedians are speaking disparagingly and sub standardly of the Dalit people for the sake of comedy. In countries like India the caste system is a very sensitive weapon so criticizing it in the name of comedy is highly misunderstood. To what extent does the critique of Dalit occur in this study? A systematic study was carried out on the extent to which the personality of the upper castes affected the lives of the common people. The study also looked at how stereotyped comedy has indirect implications. (Sivaprasad, 2020)

Research Design

This research is carried out through a qualitative research approach. Different types of comedy films have been released in Tamil at different times. But only certain Tamil comedy films are political, cultural and social reflections. The attitude of comedy films towards the social and political conditions caused by the change of time has also been changing. ImsaiArasan 23rd Pulicaci:Torture King 23rd Pulicaci (2006) and Mandela (2021) are two Tamil comedy political satire films released on average fifteen years apart. The ten-year interval is sure to have undergone various social and political changes. In the above two films, the social hierarchies and political conditions of the time when ImsaiArasan 23rd Pulicaci (2006) was released are parodied. Similarly, the Mandela film would have mocked contemporary social and political.

The purpose of this study is to examine the political satire and critique of the two films and to compare the stages of social progress and the political position over time for the two films and its position. Measured by the story and scene of the film using the text analysis method. Further comparative analysis can examine the changes over time. Both these films have won the Government of Tamil Nadu Award for Best Comedy Film. And the common denominator of these films is that it was the first film in which "Vadivelu" and "Yogi Babu", who were recorded as comedians, played the hero of the film. The data are sorted by the ideological framework of social culture and political mockery defined by story variables: plot and characteristics.

Interpretations & Analysis
Film I: ImsaiArasan 23rdPulicaci
"Kapsi" and "Akkamala"

Nixon, a British official, has come to meet King Pulicaci and collect taxes. The King of Pulicaci happily lines up for him. Nixon then asks permission from vendors to come from their country to sell soft drinks. Nixon says it also rewards 30 percent of available revenue. Permission is granted by both the King of Pulicaci and Adviser "Sangilimadan". Therefore, these drinks enter the Indian market easily. Local language actors and athletes are used to popularizing these drinks among the people. The minister will say, "This will affect local manufacturers." But the king would say, "We do not care if the local merchants are harmed, we are enjoyed 30% tax".

Soft drinks like Pepsi and Coca Cola have been renamed as Kapsi and Akkamala in the film. During the Jallikattu protest in 2017, there were many slogans that Tamil Nadu youth should ban foreign baths. Foreign drinks that are harmful to health, vowed never to drink it. Even the Tamil Nadu unions have stated that they will not sell these drinks from March 1. So, the film, which was released 15 years ago, clearly shows how these foreign energy drinks came to our market and how famous actors are used for advertising. The Indian government has allowed the sale of large quantities of foreign soft drinks without worrying about the health of the people due to the high tax and financial assistance to the country through such foreign companies. In Tamil Nadu, popular actor 'Vijay' has been appointed as the ambassador of Coca Cola. But in his film 'Kaththi' he criticizes the foreign drinks that exploit our country. Great threat to farmers who suffer for water. When asked about the controversy, he replied that he did not know about the health threats posed by these drinks when he starred in those cola commercials. Similarly, many film actors and athletes have acted as sales ambassadors.

The tyrannical rule of the king is hated by his brother *"Ukkiraputhan"*, who is an intelligent diplomat. During his reign he banned Kapsi and Akkalama and punished actors and boxers in the country. How much does a cold product cost overseas? The sellers will tell you that the cost of a cold product is 2 paise and the selling price is 10 paise. The seller will provide you genuine articles as he does not want to tarnish his own image. Ukkiraputhan who plays the king, beats him with a broom. And the high health benefits of banning those soft drinks away from coconut drinks and other beverages are being promoted by the same actors who have done it before for foreign energy.

Domain for caste conflicts

There are many problems related to caste and religion in our country. Conflicts between different castes and religions have been an important issue till now. The film parodies the caste conflicts that take place around it. In the film, two people from two different castes have been fighting in the Cholapurapalayam kingdom for about ten years. They will take this problem to the king and ask for a solution. There is only one difference between the two caste names (one caste name is "Nagapathani" and the other caste name is "Nagabpathani" only one letter 'b' is different from the other). With this they are fighting each other as one is real and the other is new and fake; They have only caste-origin and so on. King "Pulicaci" will politicize the caste issue without solving it. He will set up a caste battle ground and promote caste war without giving a proper solution.

They act as if they are superficially solving the caste problems going on in the society without coming up with a correct solution as in the movie. The Tamil Nadu government will not make noise during caste clashes and will not solve these problems for fear of losing the vote bank. Any particular caste that is ignored. They do not give the right solution to these fights as shown in the picture because they care about their welfare. The director has satirized the political situation prevailing in the state.

He also makes a nonsensical announcement. The people come to the king to resolve the issue, and he gives a different verdict, 'The new ground allotted for any caste clashes to take place from now on. At night, the battlefield is organized and the king begins to fight. He added that taxing these fights would also increase revenue. The country and your death will bring happiness to other people. So this project says when the language of success is conflicts, ethnic conflicts and conflicts related to religion will be organized separately. This particular fight depends on the financial assistance of the owners of "Gapsi" and "Akkalama". People were given these drinks during the break. Raja gives a certificate to those who are successful with job placement in government. The new emperor Ukkiraputta, who seized power, destroyed the land that had been used for caste clashes and turned it into a children's park for playing and fighting.

Arms corruption

Corruption behind arms and weapons for military personnel is a well-known phenomenon in our country. Corruption in the most important institutions, such as the military, would be a great loss to the country. When

King Pulicaci is ready for battle all the swords will break so the most frightened forces will finally show the white flag (peace flag) and pacify the enemy king before the war comes and overcome the war. Similarly, in India soldiers were given their protective clothing without proper protection, (Bullet Proof Jacket) is one of the known scams activity. So the news of the death of many soldiers came out. Politicians are behind this exploitation and benefit under everyone. Similarly, the "Rafael" flight scandal is the most talked about scandal in India. In the film, King Pulicaci punishes his servants for not using strong weapons of war.

Befriending thieves

King Pulicaci joins the thieves and makes it very difficult for the people to rob the people. The people will ask the king to catch those thieves. The king will catch two of the thieves and leave in the morning and tell the people to deal with the flock of sheep. The picture shows the kingdom ignoring the welfare of the people as it joins the thieving thieves. Many wrongdoings have taken place in India with the support of government officials and politicians. In a recent incident, a large sum of money was taken from a train with the help of police. The film shows the king's friendship with thieves and his agreement to share resources.

Isolation of Government property

There will be no elephant army in the army preparing for war, then the commander will say, "Minister, where is our elephant army? The Minister will say, "That is what we sent for rent for the wedding of the Maharaja of Travancore." Some government officials use their power to rent or sell similar state property to the private sector. During this period the government itself seeks to isolate state property. The Indian government has sold some power to the private sector.

Responsibility of government officials

i. An armed soldier is looking elsewhere without paying attention to his work while another soldier is asleep. Seeing this, King Pulikesi became angry and said, "Coming to work late in the morning, holding a spear, standing against a wall and running home in the evening, taking an hour's meal break in between, and praising it as a government job, a life like five wise lives," the king scolded. Many civil servants are still doing the above negligent work in the present times. Some government employees are these types of people, working slowly without any effort and sleeping for a while. There are such individuals in many more states. So this scene reveals parody of those people. In one scene, the king and the minister are wandering around, a soldier ordered not to do his job. The angry king wants to punish him. Then the minister becomes even more emotional and looks for his weapon that will kill him immediately. But he will not have any weapon in his clothes and forget it and come to work. So it is understandable that not only lower level government employees but also high ranking government officials are negligent donors.

ii. As well as many officers who work honestly are humiliated and subjected to assault. "Akandamuthu", who appears in the film, is the Commander-in-Chief of Pulicaci; This man did not like the activities of Pulicaci and his relationship with the British due to the arrival of energy drinks to their kingdom. He did not like the dictatorial rule of the king and he could not say a word about it. Although the kingdom is riddled with corruption and immorality, he is honest and works with Ugraputhan because he is a good king when Pulicaci's brother Ukkiraputhan comes to power. "Akandamuthu" protests against king's Pulicaci and "RajaguruSangilimayan". So when a government is full of corruption and illegal practices some employees are honest with their position but they are still under some pressure. It is not for him that "Sakayam", who brought out the IAS Madurai granite scam in Tamil Nadu, is currently working in some other field.

Film II: Mandela (2021)

The village elder, "PeriyaAyya," married two women from different castes in the Surangudi panchayat. They will contend that one caste resides in the region known as "Vadakkur," (North area) while a different caste resides in the region known as "Thekkur"(South area).The issue of caste always affects both sections. Two sons, one from the north and one from the south, were born to "PeriyaAyya" (Big Leader). Due to their selfishness, both sons will discriminate against people based on their caste and won't permit individuals to perform any basic services for their own gain.

Public toilet

In the underdeveloped village of "Surangudi", everyone seeks the environment to defecate in the morning. Although the government advertises that open defecation is harmful to the environment and the people living there, people are not properly aware of it. And moms are so poor they are not comfortable enough to build a closet. In this case, the leader of the town, "PeriyaAyya", will build a common toilet for the Surangudipanchayat. Similar to how two castes fight over using the restroom, one of the dogs will leave the restroom after defecating in it, and both castes will immediately fight over cleaning it up. To clean Smile's (Yogibabu's) closet, also known as "Ilichchavayan" and unrelated to any caste, the town's common man is called upon.

Some people engage in it for themselves in an effort to draw attention to a lower caste.But that public toilet also belongs to my caste and only those of our caste will enter the toilet first as the caste in the closet will be provoked and speak of the pride of his caste. "PeriyaAyya", who came to open the closet, will have a stroke and will fight for his life. After taking him to the hospital they would break down the toilet which was usually built during the caste war to no avail to anyone.

Many people in Tamil Nadu are suffering because of their caste, even if they have no way to eat. To provide people with shelter during the hot and rainy seasons in rural areas, the government built bus stops. However, there are an increasing number of posters at bus stops that list parties and castes. They write verses on the bus stop wall proclaiming their caste as the superior caste during caste competitions. And they'll destroy it during caste conflicts. They will immediately commit many atrocities, such as causing public disturbance and damaging public property, if there is a caste conflict. Additionally, when important government facilities (such as the Government General Hospital) are built in a caste-based area, members of the religious castes and some castes block access to those facilities. Because of caste, people cannot completely satisfy their basic needs.

Caste division based on occupation

In the village of Surangudi, a barber by the name of caste based is known as "Izhichavayan". "Kritha" is his helper and companion. He provides assistance to the villagers in a variety of ways in addition to running his shaving business. He performs a variety of tasks, such as shopping at ration stores and carrying elders' burdens. At the same time, everyone calls him out for being from a lower caste because he doesn't know his caste. He suffers public humiliation in a variety of ways, including being forbidden from entering the front door of the house and only being permitted to do so from the back, not being permitted to sit on a bus seat, and receiving physical abuse for doing so. The "Kritha" who is with him does not like all this and gets angry.

Typically, there are some people in rural areas who are not associated with any caste. He spends his life working at something that is known in that village as a source of his life, especially without knowing where he was born. People who use caste as a source of pride frequently label casteless individuals like "Izhichavayan" as belonging to a lower caste. The middle castes will treat some of the castes known as their lower caste cruelly, as mentioned above, because they accuse the upper caste of cruelty and anarchy. Even some members of so-called lower castes believe that if they belong to a lower caste, they ought to be their slaves.Caste in India was determined on the basis of occupation.It was created by Brahmins based on Varna Shastra.In the movie "Mandela", the people of the village humiliate " Izhichavayan", who works as a hairdresser, as he is a low caste based on his profession.Determining caste based on occupation is wrong.

Searching for identity

A character called "Izhichavayan" who is known by everyone in the town calls out in search of his identity without knowing his real name. He goes to the post office to save the money he has. But the postmaster denies that he cannot save money without an identity card. Then he goes to every government office for ID card. But they send him back with different reasons. The postmaster himself gives a name and applies for the identity card. The name he gives and the reason for it are important. He gives the name of "Nelson Mandela" who got the identity of his ethnic people to "Izhichawayan" who wanders in search of his identity.

In developing countries like India, individual identity is a necessity, but only a necessity, without which survival is under threat. And living without an identity card makes them look suspicious and makes them easy to criminalize. In India, various people like hill people, foxes, Tribal are still living without even an identity card, refusing the privileges of the government. But many police or government officials are harassing these people due to lack of identity. Similarly, questions have been raised about the security of the identity card. It is a very wrong thing to see a human being as two data instead of as a human being.

Election promises and caste votes

"Karunagaran", the elder of the village, falls ill and is forced to give two of his two sons a chance to run for the position of village leader in the upcoming elections. But the "Great Aiyya" is not interested in that and asks both of them a question. "What will you do to the town if you win the election? The younger son "Mathi" says that he will throw a party for our boys, take him to Goa, and convert the wine shop into a refrigerator, and throw a party in the town. Hearing this answer, the "big brother" said that both of them should not contest the elections. Because of that, he says, "If one of the two is given a chance, it will turn into a caste fight." However, despite the words of the "big brother", both of them announce that they will contest the elections.

Candidates contesting the elections will campaign by offering various concessions. If they come to power, they will make many promises like creating jobs, ensuring river connectivity, especially giving free things to the people, which has been a popular promise for some time. Some of it will be fulfilled and many will not be fulfilled. In particular, Modi said that the most expected promise to the people is that in the 2014 parliamentary elections, black money will be recovered and 15 lakh rupees will be deposited in the bank accounts of all the people of India. The above promise has been interpreted in many ways and has been subjected to many criticisms. Similarly, Mandela would have teased this promise in the movie.

Who are the good candidates for the election?

They give importance to the people of their own caste, regardless of who will help them in development. And voters are still voting on the basis of symbols and identities of senior leaders without even knowing their names. For example, in a scene in Mandela's movie, "Mathi" associates are saving a sick old woman with medical care so that she can vote. The old woman was told that one should stay alive till the election day and vote and "Who will you vote for?" He will ask. To which the old woman would say "To MGR". Immediately the shocked person will say "MGR is dead" and the old woman will die in shock.

Visually it may be normal, but the reality is that the influence of Tamil Nadu political personality leaders like MGR, Jayalalithaa, M. Karunanidhi is the choice of our previous generation even today. Moreover, rural areas will not accept the fact that MGR is dead. So they are voting based on symbols like double leaf and rising sun. Now that seems to be changing.

Selling promises for money

"You don't know how to vote but you only know how to make money by voting" is an important line in the Mandela movie. "Therkur" gives 20 rupees as a token and pays for the vote. "Vadakur" takes an oath by paying 2000 rupees in cash. Thus they pay for the vote in many ways. They decide by bidding for the vote of the protagonist (Mandela), which is considered to be an important vote. They spend up to one crore rupees per vote.

Some people expect which party will give how much money. They will sell their hole for money and complain that the government is not good. 2017 R.K. Nagar by-election TTV Dinakaran was given a token of 20 (Indian Rupee) on behalf of the party. Then the election was annulled. Some people nowadays do it as much as they can by their vote without knowing who the candidate is in their constituency.

Comparative analysis of "Imsai Arasan 23rd Pulikesi" and Mandela films

Character analysis

It is a plot with a dual character structure. Actor Vadivelu has played two roles as a king who persecutes the people and another character as a reformer. In the first part, the king who persecutes the people is set to change his mind and do good to the people through the later reform character. The self-interested king is a dual character as the public-spirited reformer. Mandela is the single character plot of the film. Common man, who belongs to any caste in the village, is a common man of the village and earns by doing the jobs that the people tell him. Yogibabu would have played an ordinary character without any authority. The desire is to build a salon of my own with the money that comes from doing the work that is available. He acts selfishly for it.

Caste related analysis

Being born in a royal family, he lives in luxury with all the comforts. Pulikesi has all the amenities that a king enjoys. He sees caste discrimination among people. The king encourages caste discrimination among them. He keeps creating agitation among people on caste. Because only then those in power can rule the country without any problems. Living in the village, Mandela is deeply affected by the influence of caste. Mandela is highly insulted by biracial people in the town. Because of the rivalry between two different castes, "Mandela" is treated as a very low caste and bullied because of the work he does.

Political Satire

Political satire is indicated as the closest match in both films. Although the movie ImsaiArasan is a story of a fictional king, the director satirically depicts many incidents and political activities along with contemporary politics. He satirized the authoritarian system very harshly. A humorous depiction of the consequences of a government failing to provide welfare programs to the people. In the second half, the ruling "Ukkiraputan" exhorts how a ruler should rule. "Pulicaci" is a ruler who does politics based on caste. He also questions the wrong view that kings can rule only if the people are kept burning with passion like caste.

The fundamental elements of Mandela's film are caste division and misguided political views. "Mandela" suffers a lot from caste exclusion and at the same time acts selfishly with the power he gets. After that, "Mandela" who changes his mind due to his bitter experience, works not for himself but for the welfare of the town. As mentioned in the movie ImsaiArasan, selfishness does not always bring happiness. Rulers should be common interest and people should also be common interest.

Reform and Public Support

In both the films after a certain period of time the protagonists of the story reform the country and the people. They know the needs of the people and fulfill them. In the movie ImsaiArasan, under the authority of the "Ukkiraputan" Arasan, he implements many programs such as education reform, caste abolition, agricultural improvement, elimination of foreign goods. Due to this, King "Pulicaci" gets a lot of admiration from the people. Only when the people feel good about the government can it be considered a good government.

According to the above, in the Mandela movie, "Mandela" who lives in the town as a sweeper is humiliated and gets his recognition through his voice, thereby fulfilling his needs. But the hero, not satisfied with his own profit, does good for the needs of the villagers. He does various welfare projects like road facility, fixing street lights, alleviating water scarcity, constructing public toilet, building a school for the village. Thus he becomes a person who can be admired by people.

Conclusion

Both these films were released almost 15 years apart. Both the films showcased various satires on caste and politics. In the period when ImsaiArasan movie was released, the political position and social position will have an impact on the cinemas of that time. The ruling methods of the rulers of that time and the social development related to the industrial development, and the reflection of the various situations prevailing in the country will be displayed in the cinema. Also, the political climate of 2006, when ImsaiArasan was released, all aspects of social development and technological progress will be depicted and satirized. An example may be the critique of caste politics.

Almost 15 years after the release of the movie "Mandela", the criticism of caste has not changed a bit. The caste politics hinted at in ImsaiArasan's film echoes in Mandela's film. Although it is proud of progress in various social progress, industrial development, technological development, the basic problems of the country have not yet been resolved. For example, we are suffering in every way like lack of food, unemployment, rising prices, increase in crime. In 2015, we are complaining about the rulers in 2006. Here, change is occurring for unnecessary reasons and excessive private gain. Both these films indicate that the view of the people has not changed and the rulers are still deceiving the people.

Reference

- Bishop, R. (2014). Comedy Cultural Critique in American Film. *UK: Edinburgh University.*
- Cherry, C. A. (2021). The Impact of Faith - Based & Comedy in Society.
- Hoon Lee, N. K. (2014). The Affect Effect of Political Satire: Sarcastic Humor, Negative Emotions, and Political Participation. *Mass Communication and Society.*
- King, G. (2002). Film Comedy. *USA: Wallflower Press.*
- Kuriakose, L. (2019). Popular shade of colourism an analysis of Humour and Body politics in Kerala's visual culture. *International Journal of Research in Humanities, Arts and Literature.*
- Lumière, L. (Director). (1895). *The Water Watered* [Motion Picture].
- Mintz, L. E. (1985). Standup Comedy as Social and Cultural Mediation. *American Quarterly , Spring, 1985, Vol. 37, No. 1, Special Issue: American.*
- Robert L. Hardgrave, J. (n.d.). The DMK and the Politics of Tamil Nationalism. *Pacific Affairs , Winter, 1964-1965, Vol. 37, No. 4 (Winter, 1964-1965),* 396-411.
- S.R. Ravikumar, K. L. (2020). A STUDY ON SYMBOLIC REPRESENTATION OF DALIT IDENTITY. *International Journal of Research in Humanities, Arts and Literature.*
- Selvan, S. (2017). An analysis on Torture King 23rd Pulikesi – A Political satire film. *Amity Journal of Media & Communication Studies (ISSN 2231 – 1033),* 65-71.
- Sivaprasad, M. (2020). Humor and the Margins: Stand-up comedy and caste in India . *IAFOR Journal of media Communication &film ,* 23-42.
- Susairaj, A. (2020). The Paradigm shifts in the Portrayal of Caste in Tamil Cinema and its impact on the Tamil Society. *Journal of the Nanzan Academic Society Humanities and Natural Sciences.*
- Thiska Septa Maiza, I. R. (2019). Racism in the Last decade of Hollywood Comedy Movies. *Journal of Transational American Studies ,* 55-70.

Film Reference

- Ashwin, M. (Director). (2021). *Mandela* [Motion Picture].
- Simbudevan (Director). (2006). *Imsai Arasan 23rd Pulicaci* [Motion Picture].

SEVEN

"FIGHT OR PLIGHT": VARIED PERSPECTIVE OF TRANS REPRESENTATION IN THE MOVIES OF EAST AND WEST VOICING THE CONCERNS OF THIRD GENDER

Prachi Malhotra

Head-Corporate Resource Centre-Amity School of Communication, Amity University-Noida

Ph.D Scholar—Amity School of Communication

Prof . Dr.Mehak Jonjua, Asst.Director (Academics)-Amity School Of Communication, Amity University-Noida

Abstract

There is no questioning to the fact that Trans genders are being portrayed negatively in movies of both East and West.Though west being less prone to Trans phobia than east where it's an obsessive fear especially in South Asia.In west also they are mocked, criticized and disliked but gradually with the onset of 21 st century and LGBTQ+movements pacing faster many people are coming out in open of their gender identity and probably being acceptedby their families. The cinema in west has also taken a turn of thoughtfulness towards this gender and movies are shifting base from mockery to solemnity. With the change of century movies in east are too raising the bar for this discarded community and showing their plight to the audience .This paper will evaluate the movie "Growing Up Coy" from Hollywood and "Darmiyan" from Bollywood to show the "Fight" for the trans genders in former and "plight" of trans genders in latter. This analysis will challenge the very root of acceptance—the family.

Keywords : Phobia, Plight, Coy

Introduction

There is no questioning to the fact that Trans genders are being portrayed negatively in movies of both East and West. Though west being less prone to Trans phobia than east where it's an obsessive fear especially in South Asia. In west also they are mocked, criticized and disliked but gradually with the onset of 21st century and LGBTQ+ movements pacing faster many people are coming out in open of their gender identity and probably being accepted by their families. The cinema in west has also taken a turn of thoughtfulness towards this gender and movies are shifting base from mockery to solemnity. With the change of century movies in east are too raising the bar for this discarded community and showing their plight to the audience .This paper will evaluate the movie "Growing Up Coy" from Hollywood and "Darmiyan" from Bollywood to show the "Fight" for the trans genders in former and "plight" of trans genders in latter. This analysis will challenge the very root of acceptance—the family.

"The family is the first essential cell of human society". This is the unit where any living being open up their eyes when they enter this world. Right from animals to Humans, what is expected from a family is to provide love, warmth, protection and care so that individual grows healthily and adapt to the world around confidently. Birth of a child brings happiness to the family .Sometimes this happiness turns gloomy due to unfortunate reasons like birth of a child with physical disformity.But parents leaves no stone unturned to medically treat their child but even then if the deformity remains they accept the child and spent their entire life in caring for this child with devotion and affection. We see around us many families where child is physically not fit but the amount of efforts parents pay is commendable, be it educated or uneducated strata of society a child is their flesh and blood. But the scenario changes drastically for this very family in our country when a child is a transgender. All hell break loose and parents are dejected as if a sin has been committed .They are sorrowful, depressed and feel downcast with shame and remorse.

Elaborating on discrimination of transgender, which begins from childhood?

NHRC (National Human Rights Commission of India) says "parents do not play a proactive role in the case of transgender children. Instead, they suffer verbal and corporal abuses at the hands oftheir parents, siblings and other family members". Most of them keep their

Identities as transgender secret till it are impossible for them to hide itforever. Most parents consider their status as physical and mental defects.Adding that transgender also do not enjoy any legal right inown theproperty inheritance. Only 2 % Transgender in India stays with their families. The irony is,it's their own family who makes them an object of disgust.

If Tran's genders are discarded by this very first social unit which is their own bloodline how can we expect the entire society to treat them normal? Ironyis, an unhealthy deformed child gets all the sympathy, care and warmth from the family but a healthy Tran's child is matter of shame and subject of hatred for the family. In our country it's mourning in the family to have a transgender as the family member. Their existence is denied and whole idea is to get over them. Whereas in our country it's a plight till date whereas in west parents are now gradually accepting the gender identity of their child which may not belong to their biological sex .They fight for their trans children to include Them in the mainstream. "Growing Up Coy" is one such story where as "Darmiyan" shows the Indian side of it.

Rationale of the Study

"Charity Begins at Home". This proverb has a very in depth meaning. If we can't get our house set, we should not expect anything from the society. Transgender are hated and ostracized by the society primarily because their own family discardsthem. Transphobia can be erased and trans genders can be included in mainstream as government as legal body is bringing out lot of policies for them but this all is in vain because the first cell of human society i.e. the family is in non-acceptancemode If the family is strong enough to stand by their side, society will gradually come to terms with it.

Objective

To study and compare the treatment of Trans genders by the parents of East and West when the gender identity of their child beyond the normal biological sex is disclosed to them.

Research Questions

1. Can support of parents and family help in reducing transphobia?

2. How family can play a vital role in normalizing the life of theirTrans members and make them acceptable by the civil society?

Research Methodology

Content analysis of two movies "Growing up Coy" (Hollywood) and "Darmiyan" (Bollywood).

Analysis and Findings

Over the course of several years in Colorado, the movie "GROWING UP COY" follows Jeremy and Kathryn Mathis and their five kids. One young transgender girl, Coy Mathis, age 6, who came out in kindergarten, is one of the kids. Up until the first grade, she was permitted to use the girls' restroom without restriction. However, the principal then notified the parents that going forward; Coy would only be permitted to use the boys' restroom or the nurse's restroom. Jeremy and Kathryn withdrew their children from school rather than comply, and they collaborated with the Transgender Legal Defense & Education Fund to lodge a complaint with the Colorado Civil Rights Division.

The Mathises made their case public while they awaited a ruling, which attracted attention to the problem in a global media frenzy, while they awaited a ruling, the Mathises made their case public and became a focal point for the controversy in global media frenzy, making noteworthy appearances on Katie and getting a spread in Rolling Stone. The movie then depicts how Jeremy and Kathryn's marriage suffered due to media pressure, ultimately resulting in their separation. Finally, a decision in their favor was made, allowing transgender people all around the state to use facilities that correspond to their gender identity.

The decision, which was a first for the United States, had tremendous impact on the entire nation. California passed a bill allowing transgender students to choose the bathrooms and sports teams they choose soon after the decision.For nondiscrimination, the Obama Administration released rules to safeguard transgender students. The majority of the so-called bathroom bills, which would require transgender students to use the restroom that matches their birth certificates, were proposed by many states in opposition to the rules. One restroom measure, HB2 in North Carolina, has so far become a law.

Now if we analyse DARMIYAN with a brief where the protagonist ZeenatBegum is a well-known actress who dominates the movie business and is opulent in every way. Zeenat's joy is sadly dashed when she learns that her son Emmi is a eunuch. In public, she refers to him as her younger brother and denies that he is her son. She begins a romance with Inder Kumar Bhalla, a budding actor , only to lose him to Chitra, a younger actress, years laterZeenat eventually loses her top spot in the film industry to Chitra and experiences depression. She turns to alcoholism and starts to turn away from the ones she loves. While anxiously fending off Champa, a Hijra head, Emmi desperately tries to assist his distraught mother.

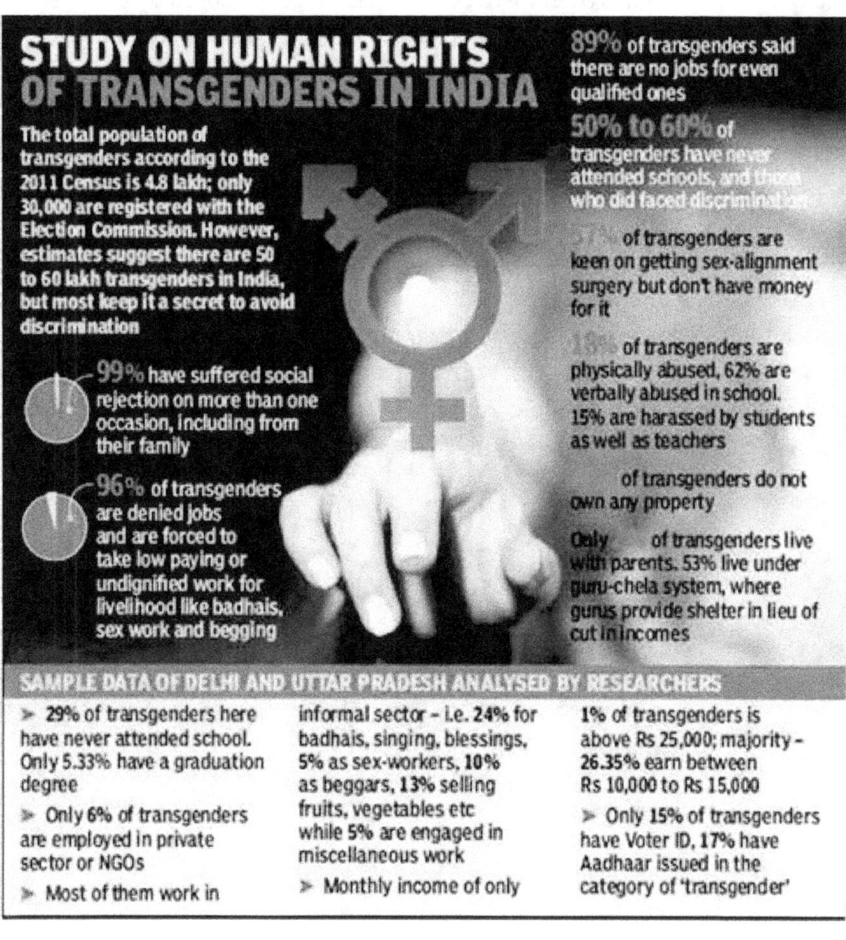

Image Credit : Author

Conclusion

The central idea behind growing up coy is that how a transgender can cross hurdles in life when they have rock solid and unconditional support of their family. Coy's parents also suffered a great personal pain but eventually they won the war in support of their Trans child that new laws were framed. Such is the strength of the family. Whereas in Darmiyan , a mother is in denial of her Trans child's existence and refuses to even accept him. The child eventually takes care of her ,who was never welcomed by the family and lived a sad and unhappy life.

Recommendation

Transgender should be accepted by their families .This will help them to lead a normal life. As per the NHRC survey (2016) only 2 percent Trans genders live with their parents and rest others enters prostitution/begging. 99% Trans genders suffer social rejections.Outsed from home they enter the GURU-CHELA system for survival and pick up petty jobs.With the warmth and care of the family they can be much better and can gel in the society well, gradually there will acceptance and less of phobia.

Reference

https://timesofindia.indiatimes.com/india/left-alone-just-2-of-trans-people-stay-with-parents/articleshow/65380226.cms

EIGHT
DUB MOVIES AND CHANGES IN MILLENNIAL

Anuj Dr. Dheeraj Kumar

Research Scholar Assistant Professor

Department of Mass Communication Department of Mass Communication

Mizoram University Mizoram University

thanujpratap@gmail.com dheeraj@mzu.ac.in

Abstract

Movies are good medium of entertainment and infotainment. In exceptional cases various movies create tension between society, community and nations etc. Theodore Aderno (1947) says that media is a cultural industry. So dub movies are also cause of changes and these changes can be positive and negative. These cultural changes also consider good or bad on the basis of frame of reference. This study will try to explore, how millennial are changing after the dubbing culture in India. These changes can be based on various aspects such as linguistic, shopping habit, behavior etc. this study is qualitative study and sub type of study is descriptive. According to nature and requirement of the study. Researcher will follow mixed method approach. Universe of this study will be millennial of Delhi-NCR. Sampling frame for this study is who watch the dub movies. Number of sample size will be 50. Questionnaire will be used as a tool of data collection. Data will be analyzed by the help of SPSS.

Keywords: Frame of reference, Millennial, cultural industry, infotainment

Introduction

The Indian film industry produces more movies as compared to other film industries in the world. Based on money Indian film industry is on the second rank after Hollywood. The Indian film industry can exist in more than 90 countries. India ranked number two based on population, so people watch here cinema of the entire world. Indian cinema means all types of cinema India Hindi, Tamil, Telugu, Malayalam and Kannada and Bhojpuri and Marathi cinema, etc. Dubbing cinema is also in trend people are watching other cinemas after dubbing in Indian languages. Hindi language cinema has a huge fan following base. In Indian cinema, there are two types of dubbing movies. Bollywood produced 1500 to 2000 cinemas per year (Selvalakshmi et al., 2020). The first type of cinema is Indian regional cinema this dubbed in Hindi and Hindi movies are also dubbed in regional languages. The second type of cinema is foreign cinema is dubbed in Indian languages. In this study, dubbing means Hollywood cinema dubbed in the Hindi language. Cinema is a very big industry, and it provides various jobs in direct and indirect ways.

Movies are various types, and every movie has a different impact on society, individuals, and community and sometimes its impact on countries and worldwide. Every country has a different type of certification authority that certifies the cinema. These certifications are mandatory for all types of cinemas like a country-made or foreign cinema. In India, there is a body that certifies the cinema Central Board of Film Certification. These certifications are given to every cinema according to their content and target audience. In India, these certificates are mandatory to show before starting the film. Movies can create social benefits. Dangal, Secret Superstar and Toilet: Ek prem Katha, etc. these movies change the society and mentality of patriarchal society. These films worked well in women empowerment and gender equality. (Uday et al., 2018).

Generations

The basis of differentiating generations is the place of birth. These generations differ in different ways from one another. Despite the fact that everyone has the same culture, it is always evolving. Each generation has some qualities. According to the Pew Research Center a generation is supposed to consist of people who were born between the ages of 15 and 20. This study describes how to compare generations through time to see how people have evolved. The term "Gen X" refers to the people who were born between 1965 and 1980. The Gen X generation is thought to be resourceful, self-reliant, and eager to combine work and personal life. Baby Boomers are the generation born between 1946 and 1964. They belonged to the Baby Boomer group, which emerged after World War I. People who were born between 1980 and 1998 are referred to as millennial or Generation Y. The amount millennial owes on their home loans have increased by 10% as house prices and interest rates have gone up. People born between 1997 and the present are referred to as Generation Z. Each of us as a individual we are different in many ways such as ethnicity, race, sexual orientation, gender, socioeconomic etc. these dimensions together create our frame of reference. With the help of frame of dereference we create and interpret message.

Review of literature

(Editor & Caton, 2021) The trend of translated films has increased rapidly in India. Translation of films is a very complex process. Most Hollywood movies are translated into Hindi. In the translation of films, efforts are made to use colloquial language instead of bookish language. Just as filmmaking is a complex process and requires the labor of many people, similarly the help of many experts is taken in the translation of the film. Culture is also taken into account in the translation of the film. There is a big market for translated films in India, it is mostly seen in the Hindi belt. Due to the craze for translated films in India, many films are released simultaneously around the world.

(Patel, 2019) The generation of man is divided into several parts according to the order of birth. Some positive and negative aspects of all these generations have also been told by experts. People born between 1946 and 1964 are called Baby Boomers, those born in the 1965 to 1980s are called Generation X, and those born between 1981 and 2000 are called Millennial. Millennial have been included in this study.

- (Naz et al., 2018) find in the study in Effects of Hindi dubbed cartoons on students' linguistic patterns and culture, Cartoons are the main means of entertainment; children spend most of their time watching cartoons. For the past decade, foreign cartoons are translated into Hindi language and shown to children. Due to the increasing demand for foreign cartoons in India, now the Indian festivals are also being given preference in the cartoons translated in Hindi. Social cognitive theory has been used in this research. It has also been found in this study that many changes are also coming in children due to cartoons. At this young age, children are able to learn easily. This program is designed keeping people in mind. With this, the children who are now growing up are also learning the words of many cultures.

- (Satpute et al., 2022)This study shows that now technological changes are happening very fast in the world. These changes are affecting all dimensions of life. The world of films, cartoons and television etc. is no longer untouched by it. Now along with animation, artificial human sounds are also being used in making programs. All this has been made possible by artificial intelligence and deep learning. Nothing is deep fake but it is not real either. Images are created through deep fakes as well as videos which do not exist in reality. This deep fake video makes a lot of impact on people. Deep fake videos are used more with educational videos, if there is a technical flaw in it then the lipping does not match. It has also been told in this study that in this era of globalization, this technology is going to spread a lot.

- (ABDERRAZAG & Kazi-Tani, 2018) This study has found that translated films have an impact on the audience. This study also states that Marshall McLuhan's theory of Global Village fits perfectly in today's time. One end of the world is connected to the other due to technological development. Through this technology, translated programs are now being sent from one country to another to see how the translation of Turkish programs is affecting the decisions, thoughts and behavior of the people of Algeria. This study explained that programs that we consider appropriate for children, especially programs that are from other countries and are being shown to children. This program also affects the ability of children to make decisions as they grow up. The government needs to make such programs rules.

- (Kumar & Kumar Mohapatra, 2020) It has been found in this research that now people do not like television programs under pressure. Due to this the trend of web series is increasing. With the increasing pace of web series in India, now foreign series are also being translated into Indian languages. Many web series from India have touched the ladder of fame like Sacred Games, Mirzapur, Rangbaaz etc. Technological change has made all this much faster and easier. The study found that some people want the government not to make any strict rules regarding online content and language, but this content is spoiling the language of the youth. The future of web series in India is bright because India is a country of youth and the number of youth here is sufficient.

- (Hong, 2021) It has been told in this research that India is also identified in the world with Bollywood, which is based in Mumbai. It is also known for producing the largest number of films in the world. Today Indian cinema, especially Bollywood cinema, has a reach in every corner of the world. The craze of Bollywood movies can also be seen in China. It has been told in this research paper that China also has cultural ties with India, due to which Hindi films are given priority in China, all this is happening at a time when the situation between the two countries on the border also becomes tense. Is. Is. Bollywood produces the largest number of films in the world but Hollywood leads in terms of box office collections. Bollywood is being seen as a soft power in China due to Indian music, dance, recognition etc. Many subject matter experts are seeing this as cultural globalization and some even as cultural imperialism. China is the second largest film market in the world after the US. China's film business is difficult to capture because of the quota system, which can only show 34 foreign films a year. China's craze for Indian films is not a hasty process, but people have been crazy about Bollywood cinema since the 1980s. Chinese President Xi Jinping told Prime Minister Narendra Modi at the 2017 summit that he liked Aamir Khan's Dangal. Aamir Khan is called 'Mi Shu' i.e. 'Uncle Mi' in China. More than 32 interviews were conducted for this research.

- (*Ritual, Romance, and Royalty: Bollywood Remakes of Hindu Femininity - ProQuest*, n.d.) This research paper states that Bollywood has always been an important center between India and Indians living in any corner of the world. The festivals of India are expanding through Indian films. The festival of Karva Chauth was earlier celebrated in some parts of India, now this festival is celebrated through media all over India. Now this festival is being celebrated among the Indians settled in the world including India and it is also affecting the natives of those countries. India is promoting and spreading its culture in the world through media. Indianans is expanding slowly but in every corner of the world where Indians are living.

- (Patel, 2019) This study states that generations are divided on the basis of their year of birth. This division is used in various studies. This genetic division is now used as a scale. There are five types of generations that can be seen in any workplace today. Conservatives, Baby Boomers, Generation X, Millennial (or Generation Y), and Generation Z. In all these generations, Millennial have garnered the most attention as their aspirations and needs have been higher than the rest. By genetic order, the successors of Baby Boomers were Millennial. A generation is a group that is programmed at one time and in the same period of history. Baby Boomers 1946–1964, Generation X 1965–1980, Millennial 1981–2000. Millennial were the heirs of Baby Boomers. He grew up with technology and grew up with a group and gave more time to the group. This generation is also a product of social liberalism. He also saw unpleasant economic growth. Millennial are fully aware of their purpose. He is more attached to his job and society.

Rationale of the study

'Culture Industry: Enlightenment as Mass Deception' this is a chapter in a book called "Dialectic of Enlightenment", authored by Theodor Adorno & Max Horkheimer. The market is regulated as an instrument. Culture Industry means the production of goods on a large scale. This theory of the Frankfurt School explains how the people are exploited through the capitalist system. A capitalist society brings about some changes in the culture. The cultural industry gives cultural products to the people in the name of consumer products. Culture is transformed into a commodity through painting, cinema, and literature. The group that sells the cultural product gives less importance to creativity, and ideas than to the creation and item. Their primary objective is to make the individual an indirect consumer and also influence their ability to make their own decisions. Cultural industries provide easy entertainment, then exploited by the upper class. The principle of the market is based on product and demand, where the demand is controlled and then the demand is also controlled. Instead of traditional music, pop music tells people about the physical world along with the music. The same happens with TV, serials, their messages change with time, but they also promote the cultural industry in a changed form. It has also been told in this theory that with the changing times a person has lost a lot such that his own freedom is now under the control of the market.

Research Objectives

RO1: To examine the importance of dubbed movies.

RO2: To find out the need for dubbed movies.

RO3: To know whether movies are acting on people like catalysts.

Research Questions

RQ1: Why youth are getting attracted to the foreign cinema?

RQ2: Has the marketing trends of dubbed movies changed or not? RQ3: How cinemas work as element of cultural industry?

RQ4: Cinema supports a specific culture, so are dubbed movies made keeping these things in mind?

Research Methodology

Quantitative method has been used in the present research study. Descriptive research is used as a sub-type of research. Quantitative method has been used as a research approach. Millennial are included in the universe of research. In the sampling frame, people who watch movies translated in Hindi have been kept. Movies of all languages translated in Hindi have been included in this frame. The data will be compiled through online questionnaire of data collection. Sample size was 100 and area of data collection was Delhi-NCR.

Data Interpretation

Q1. Interpretation: Out of the whole target audience, 63% are male respondents 37% are females. The majority of the respondents are between the age of 25- 27 years old, and every respondent is interested in watching movies.

Age	Percentage
33	3%
30	4%
31	4%
24	6%
26	6%
29	6%
23	9%
32	13%
25	15%
28	15%
27	19%

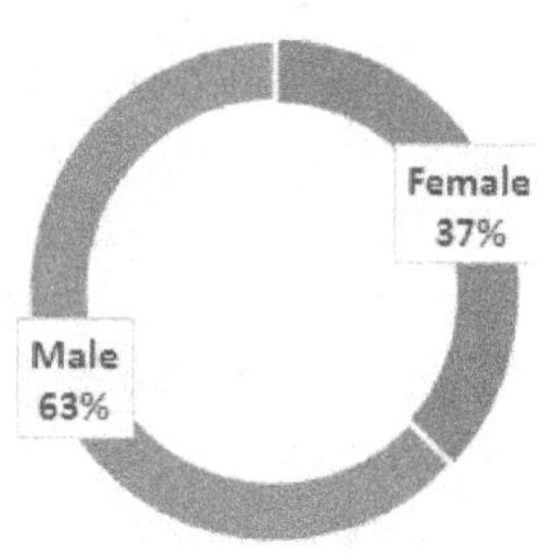

Q2. Interpretation: The table given below shows that 49% of the respondents watches movies once a week while only 20% watches movies regularly.

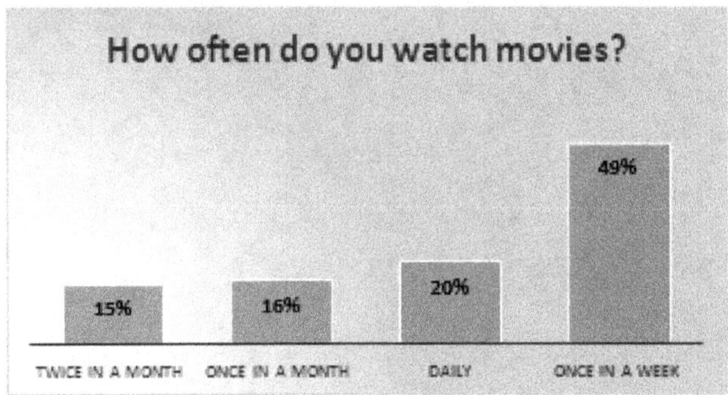

Q3. Interpretation: According to below- mentioned table, there is a high percentage who are likely to watch "All Indian Cinema" (32%), as well as 28% of people who have indicated that they liked Bollywood movies, whereas 24% have watched Hollywood and South Indian movies percentage is 16.

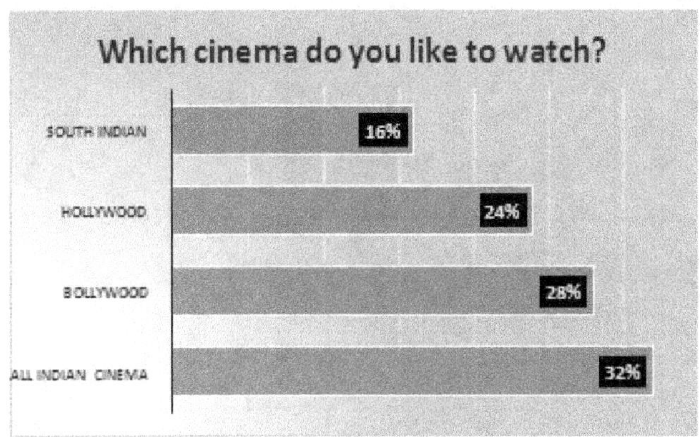

Q4. Interpretation: The majority of people have watched Dubbed movies, and there are only 6% of people haven't watched Dubbed movies which are showing that people are more aware of these movies and also, they are interested to watch.

Have you ever watched dubbed movies?

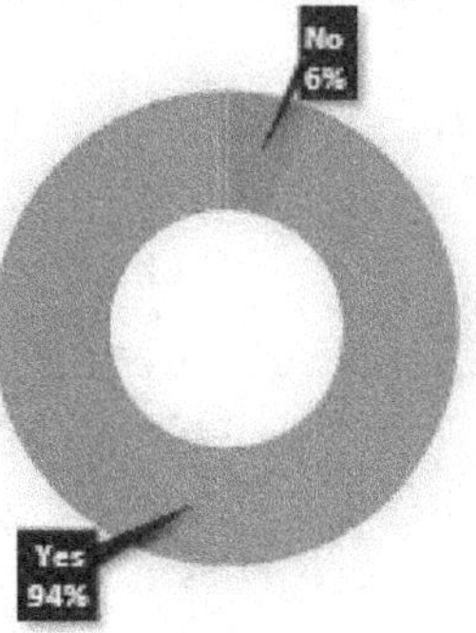

Q5. Interpretation: People who watch dubbed movies, a majority, around 41% say the story of a movie attracts them a lot as compared to Indian Cinema while 23% of indicating that they like all the above-mentioned features like Music, Animation, VFX, Dialogues, Voice, and Actions.

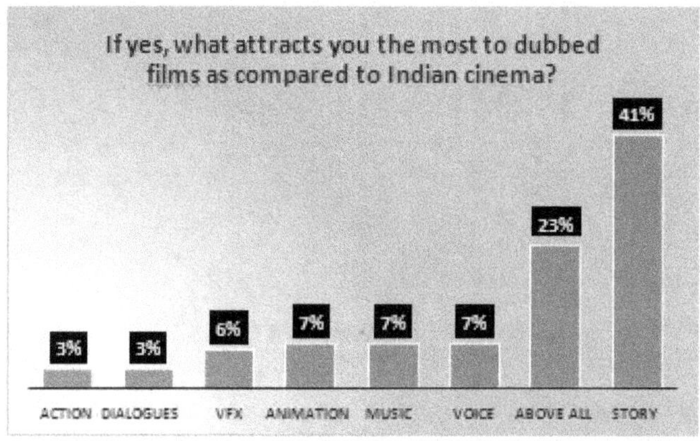

Q6. Interpretation: Nearly, 68% of respondents admitted that Dubbed movies are affecting the Indian Culture while 32% say No.

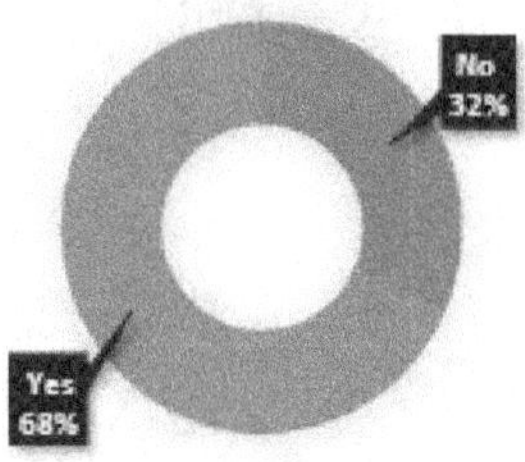

Q7. Interpretation: Approximately 61% of people mention that dubbed movies have both the impacts positive and negative. Also, 34% show a positive impact.

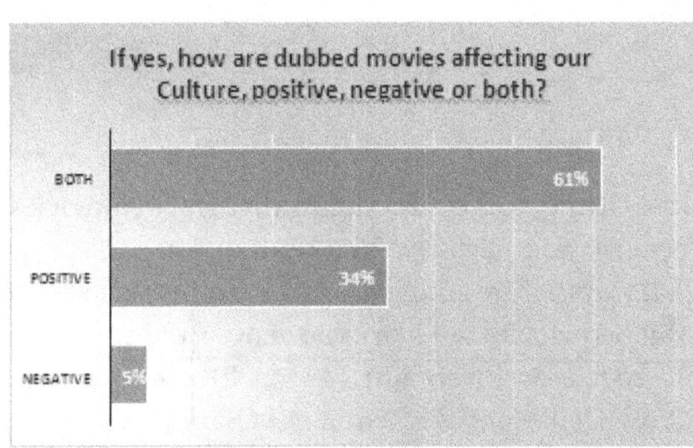

Q8. Interpretation: Almost 59%, have mentioned that Dubbed movies introduce us to other cultures in our own mother tongue, while the same percentage of 14% people mention that from Dubbed movies, they get knowledge about other cinema movies and it also shows the glory of India, especially South and Maharashtrian cinema and rest of the people admit that it gets knowledge about the other culture.

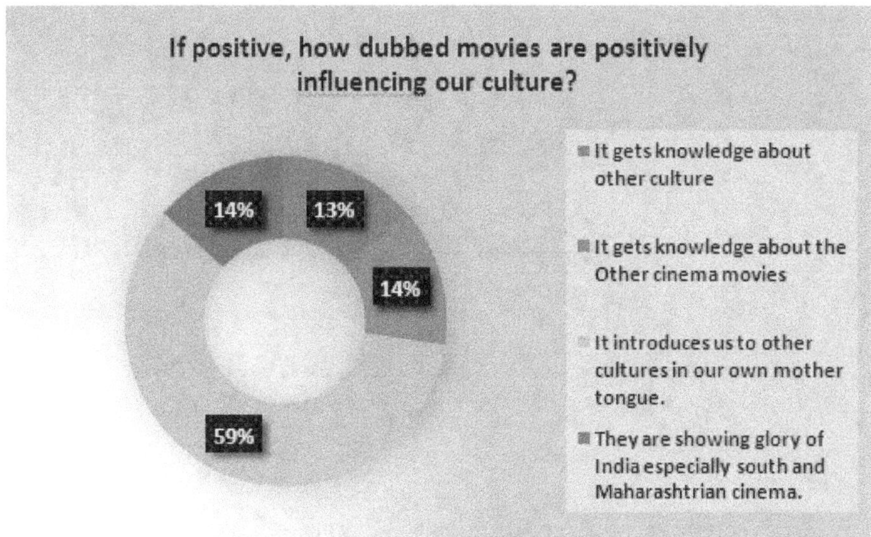

Q9. Interpretation: Of the people who admit that Dubbed movies have both the impacts positive and negative, 26% of people say that it always depends on us in what ways we are taking it positively or negatively whereas 23% mention that Dubbed movies are like other movies only. Just language dubbing is there. It affects positively just like an RRR movie, it awakes you about your culture. Hollywood dubbed movies have an impact on our culture. Other 18% of people have mentioned that sometimes the impact is positive or negative while 10% say that in every culture, there is something to learn.

If both, how dubbed movies are influencing our culture?	Percentage%
Depends on how we are taking it	26%
Dubbed movies are like other movies only. Just language dubbing is there. It affects positively RRR, it awakes you about your culture. Hollywood dubbed movies have an impact on our culture.	23%
Sometimes the impact is positive and sometimes is negative	18%
In every culture, there is something to learn	10%
Gives a window to understanding foreign culture and also it depends on movie to movie	8%
Influencing by showing the culture of related community or religion in actual form in the reel, somewhere they are near to actuality somewhere they are not.	8%
Values and traditions which are presented in the movies and family relationships as now we are restricted to ourselves	8%

Q10. Interpretation: This chart indicates that the majority of people know that dubbed movies are adapted according to the Indian audience while 26% say No.

Q11. Interpretation: Approximately 86% of people get influenced and wanted to buy the products after watching dubbed movies and only 14% of people don't want to buy any product which is a very less percentage.

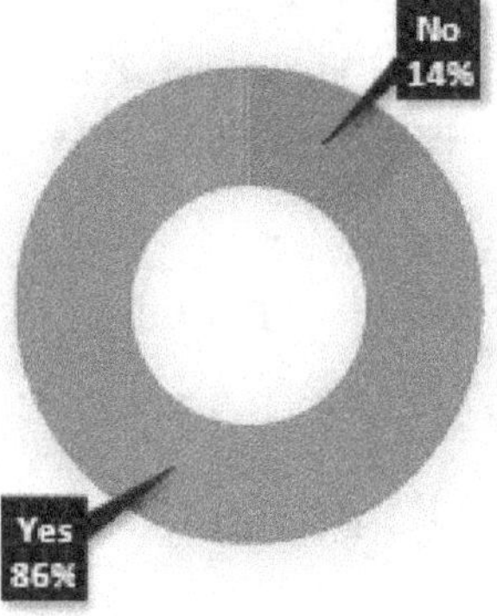

Q12. Interpretation: The below-mentioned chart shows that a high proportion of people around 60%, indicates that they have evaluated any dabbed movies based on the storyline. Only 20% of people mention the language and a very less percentage of people evaluate dubbed movies on the basis of Graphics and Visuals.

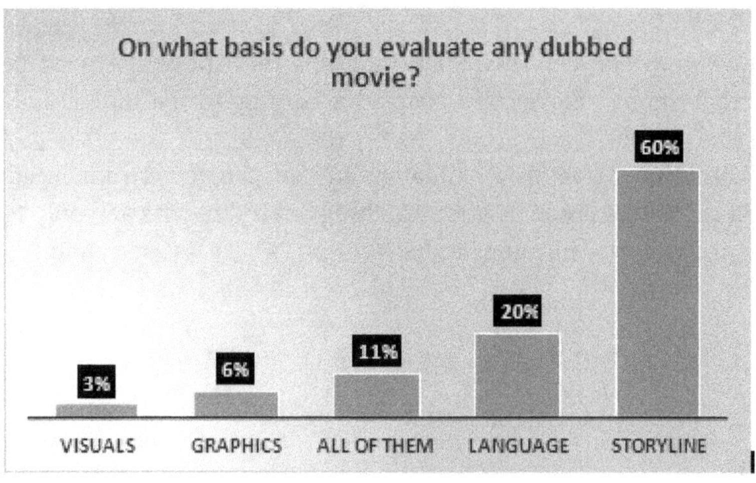

Findings

As a result of the study, generally, people watch movies and people mostly prefer to watch movies once in a week. The obtained results are showing that people watch all Indian Cinema whether it is Bollywood, South Indian movies, or others. This study revealed that people form an opinion of dubbed movies on the basis of their stories. From this study, the researcher has concluded that dubbed movies are affecting our culture and have both impacts Positive and Negative. The positive aspect is that from dubbed movies people get knowledge of other cultures and the negative aspect is that Hollywood movies have a bad impact on our culture. Dubbed movies feature specific products and services along with their content. These products and services are reflected, directly and indirectly, in their content. These programs cause desire in the minds of the target audience. The viewer is also inclined to buy these goods and services directly or indirectly. This type of work these industries act as a tool of cultural industries.

References

Naz, S., Rasheed, M., & Rasheed, T. (2018). Effects of Hindi Dubbed Cartoons on Students' Linguistic Patterns and Culture. Global Language Review, III(I), 126–135. https://doi.org/10.31703/glr.2018(iii-i).08

Satpute, H., Raut, S., Sapke, P., & Dixit, M. (2022). Deepfake Creation Using Generative Adversarial Network. 8(6), 360–372.

ABDERRAZAG, S. H., & Kazi-Tani, L. (2018). The Negative Influence of Turkish Series' Dubbing on Algerian Adolescents. Journal of English Language and Literature, 10(3), 1039. https://doi.org/10.17722/jell.v10i3.410

Kumar, S., & Kumar Mohapatra, A. (2020). An Analytical Study of Content and Language of Indian Webs Series. Journal of Xi'an University of Architecture & Technology, 12(5), 919–930.

Hong, Y. (2021). The power of Bollywood: A study on opportunities, challenges, and audiences' perceptions of Indian cinema in China. Global Media and China, 6(3), 345–363. https://doi.org/10.1177/20594364211022605

Ritual, Romance, and Royalty: Bollywood Remakes of Hindu Femininity - ProQuest. (n.d.). Retrieved September 19, 2022, from https://www.proquest.com/openview/dbc4e374f72df34c200e4f03fc376b78/1?pq- origsite=gscholar&cbl=646376

Patel. (2019). Examining Generational Differences in The Workplace: Employee Engagement Practices and their Impact on Retention of Different Generations of Human Resources Employees. 9–25.

Pew Research Center. (2015). *The Whys and Hows of Generations Research | Pew Research Center.* https://www.pewresearch.org/politics/2015/09/03/the-

<u>whys-and-hows-of-</u> generations-research/

What years are Gen X, baby boomers, millennials, Gen Z_ What to know. (n.d.).

Bobbitt, R. (2020). An Overview of Communication Ethics. *Exploring Communication Ethics*, 1–24. https://doi.org/10.4324/9780429324475-1

NINE

LAND OF SNAKE CHARMERS TO THE LAND OF UNICORNS: THE ROLE OF SOFT POWER DIPLOMACY IN CREATION OF A NEW GLOBAL IMAGE OF INDIA

Prabhat Kumar, Research Scholar,
   Department of Mass Communication & Journalism,
   Tezpur University, Assam, 784028

Abstract

Countries, large and small, are now keenly aware that their image and reputation can be vital strategic resources in world affairs (Wang, 2011). Thus every nation desires to have a positive global image which will help them to pursue their nationalinterests in the global geopolitical system. India's imagejust after itsindependence was that of a weak and oppressed nation incapable of helping itself; a nation heavily dependent on others for economic and food aids. But in the last 75 years the country has made a long journey from being seen as an impoverished third world nation to becoming fifth largest economy of the world. India is no more seen as a land of snake charmers rather it is seen as a land of unicorns. It is seen as a majorrising global power. The tools of India's soft power diplomacy such as yoga, meditation, spirituality, Bollywood, culture, cuisines,fairs,festivals, dance forms, music and diversity have played a great role in construction of a positive image of the country.This paper aims toexamine the kind of frames that have been used to look at India in thepast and how they have changed in the present times. How the world views India today and what is the role of soft power diplomacy in defining India's global image are the issues which have been explored in the paper.

Keywords : India, Diaspora, Rising Global Power, Soft Power, Cultural Diplomacy

Introduction

In the colonial period India was perceived as the land of snake charmers, tigers, elephants and beggars (Machaiah, 2019).Similar observations are made by British journalist Miller (2014) according to whom India was seen as a land of Maharajas and rope tricks; tigers and diamonds; snake charmers and Taj Mahal. For Lord Macaulay, it was a nation whose entire native literature was not "worth a single bookshelf of Western writing" and to Winston Churchill, it was "a beastly country with a beastly religion" (Luce, 2008). The negative image and stereotyping led to the common belief that India was an ancient, uncivilized, backward, primitive nation steeply rooted in its traditions and past but miles away from modernity.The colonial rulers were of the firm opinion that Indians did not have the capability to govern themselves. If India was left to its own fate then it would create anarchy hence it was a nation which needed to be civilized by the white men.

Colonial India's this kind of representation can be best seen in the famous Hollywood movieIndiana Jones and the Temple of Doom (1984). According to Tharoor (2012) this movie depicted India in a very poor light as a country where kings and courtiers feasted on stewed snakes and monkey brains, where Kali worshippers plucked the hearts out of their victims and embroiled them in flaming pits and where evil, poverty and destitution reigned.Famous American historian and journalist Katherine Mayo who published her book titled 'Mother India' in 1927 attacked the Indian society, religion and culture and advanced the case of continued British rule in India

(Raghavan,2018). Her book presented image of India as a poverty stricken land of strange and debilitating sexual mores to the western audience (Miller, 2014).

The long colonial rule left the nation with huge economic underdevelopment, gross poverty, near total illiteracy, wide prevalence of diseases, stark social inequality and injustice. Sinceits independence in 1947 India's journey in last 75 years has been fascinating. In year 2022 India has become the fifth largest economy of the world and as per Galloway(2020) by 2050, India is projected to be the world's second-largest economy (overtaking the United States) and will account for 15% of the world's total GDP. It aims to become $5 trillion economy in the coming years.

The best thing about India's economic growth is that according to a report published by United Nations India lifted 271 million people out of poverty between 2006 and 2016 (PTI, 2019). The country today is getting recognition as the land of unicorns (start-up companies touching a valuation of more than $1 billion).Havingthe third largest start-up ecosystem in the world India of 2022 is a confident nation full of possibilities.In global Ease of Doing Business Index it has improved to 63rd position (in 2019) from 134th position (in 2013) there by making business and investments in India much easier than before. India is home to some of the best IT companies in the world like Wipro, TCS, Infosys, Tech Mahindra. Indian corporate houses like Tata, Reliance, Adani Group, Vedanta, Airtel are some of the biggest investors and job providers in many countries.

Mukherjee & Malone (2011) observed that India's voice carries more weight today in multilateral forums largely due to its enhanced economic power, political stability, and nuclear capability. India is a member of important global bodies and institutions such as BIMSTEC, BRICS, Commonwealth, G 20, IAEA, IMF, World Bank, MTCR,NAM, SAARC, SCO etc. India is an active member of Quad and aspires to become a permanent member of United Nations Security Council. India has also joined a middle eastern Quad with Israel, UAE and US and continues to be one of the major contributors of troops for UN peacekeeping missions (Pande, 2017).

In the Covid 19 pandemic period India reinforced its global image of being called as the pharmacy of the world. Serum Institute of India led in vaccine production (Covishield) and supplied it across the globe. According to a report since the start of Vaccine Maitri Programme in January, 2021, India supplied 723.435 lakh doses of Covid vaccine to 94 countries and to two UN entities in the form of grant, commercial export or through COVAX till November 29, 2021(PTI, 2021). It also supplied hydroxychloroquine, paracetamol, PPE and diagnostic kits to the nations in need.

In the field of space science India achieved the feat of becoming the first Asian nation to send a mission to Mars in 2014. It achieved this in its maiden attempt that too at the lowest cost (₹450 Crore only). Similarly,in the area of environment and climate change much progress has been made with special focus on renewable energy. At the 26th Conference of Parties (CoP26), Indian Prime Minister Narendra Modi declared that by the year 2070, India will achieve the target of Net Zero emissions. In 2015 PM Modi along with French president Francois Hollande launched the International Solar Alliance to promote solar energy in 121 tropical countries (Krishnakutty, 2021).

In a nutshell it can be said that India is no more a Third world and backward country but rather a strong economic, political and military power. But it is not just the hard power aspects where India has excelled but the contribution of soft power of India has been equally important in its growth and earning of global goodwill. Similarly, Indian cinema specially Bollywood has a wide global appeal. Indian cuisines and restaurants enjoy popularity globally. This paper tries to explore the role of India's soft power diplomacy in creating a positive global image for the country.

Literature Review

Pradhan & Mohapatra (2020) observe that though there was an increase in recognition given to Indian diaspora but they was no serious attempt to incorporate this phenomenon into India's foreign policy formulation process until recently. Diaspora act as a form of soft power for India. They help in shaping and influencing the domestic and foreign policies of India. Diaspora have also contributed immensely in the economic development of India.

Mazumdar (2018) observed India's soft power diplomacy as practiced by the Modi government in the post 2014 period. He argues that Modi administration laid more emphasis on three aspects which were Buddhism, Diaspora and Yoga as part of soft power diplomacy and they have been used as tools to pursue specific interests and goals in the area of foreign policy.

Mahapatra (2016) reflected on India's evolution from a latent to a 'strong' soft power and the role played by cultural diplomacy in this process. He suggests that Indian leadership in the recent times focused more on its diaspora, multicultural ethos, and its ancient practices like yoga, through official campaigns and foreign visits. He gives the example of how Modi government in 2014 tried to build a consensus in the United Nations to adopt 21st June as International Yoga Day.

Thussu (2016) looked at how global popularity Indian cinema acted as one of the key soft power tools for India.He notes that among the BRICS nations, India has the most developed and globalised film industry. Indian government as well as corporations have been increasingly deploying the power of Bollywood in their international interactions. The globalisation of the country's popular cinema was aided by a large diaspora and had huge possibilities of promoting India's public diplomacy.

Mukherjee (2014) says that although there has been a steady increase in writing on India's soft power however, in terms of impact, Indian soft power has fallen far short of expectations. He notes that significant sections of public opinion in the West and in Asia are still not favourable toward India. He is doubtful and cynical about any significant role played by soft power in India's diplomatic gains since the early 1990s.

Hall (2012) found that in recent years India was trying to use traditional as well as new approaches to build and leverage its soft power. His study looks at different forms of public and cultural diplomacy used by India and their effectiveness in shaping public opinion. The study claims that Indian investment in public diplomacy was partially a response to the growth of Chinese soft power and partially due to the emergence of social media.

Kugiel (2012) studied how India was trying to spread soft power in the South Asian region. According to himasymmetrical power relations and India's contested leadership in South Asia were two major impediments in ensuring peace and stability in this region. He feels that there are limitations to the hard power approach and therefore India wanted to go forsoft power to earn goodwill in the region. Soft power tools and cultural diplomacy have helped it to rebuild its positive image and attract more neighbours into a vision of shared prosperity and peace.

Blarel (2012)in his study found that scholars and analysts until now mostly focused on material indicators such as economic growth, military expansion or demographic evolution which were all the various aspects of hard power. What was being overlooked in the process was India's increasing emphasis on developing its 'soft power' in form of Indian culture, values and policies, food, music, technology and Bollywood. The study argues that India's soft power resources have actually helped strengthen India's global status. Hemonitors the evolution of India's soft powerand compares it with the efforts made by China in this regard.

Wagner (2010) studied India's soft power, its prospects and limitations and found that the rich democratic tradition, legacy of Mahatma Gandhi and his idea of non-violence and Bollywood were some natural elements of India's soft power. In addition to it India's high economic growth rate post 1991 also made it an attractive destination for the investors. According to him India is more of a defensive soft power unlike US and China.

Research Questions

RQ 1. What are the key elements of India's soft power diplomacy?

RQ 2. How do these elements continue to shape India's foreign policy and its global image?

Methodology

This is basically a review paper based on secondary data. Information has been obtained from various sources such as books, magazines, newspaper articles and research papers. Since image evolution is a very gradual process therefore in this studymore focus has been paid on how India's global image has been changing in the recent times. The conceptual framework which has been used in the article is the concept of soft power given by Joseph Nye Jr. in 1990.

Discussion

According to Joseph Nye soft poweris the ability *of a country to persuade others to do what it wants without force or coercion. It* has become one of the key means to success in present day world politics for nation states. It is as important as hard power (political, military, economic) in International Relations. According to him *soft power of a nation depends on three things: its* culture, its political values and its foreign policies.Soft power helps to form national image which is the sum total of impressions and opinions people of one nation have towards the people and governments of other nations.Image of a nation is formed due to various factors like society, culture, values, economy and politics. According to Lodhi (2021) a positive country image can play crucial role in earning respect and increase the nation's weight in international affairs. It also helps to attract investors, tourists, international students, donors etc.Whereas nations with a negative image and perception face great difficulty to pursue their interests on world stage.

Key Elements of India's Soft power

1. **Diaspora**

With a strength of 18 million people the Indian diaspora is largest in the world. This diaspora is vibrant, dynamic and spread across all the continents. India is the world's biggest recipient of remittances sent by its diaspora. In 2021 this amount was$87 billion. Indian diaspora has helped India toearn prestigeand goodwillabroad. Pande (2017)observes that Indian diaspora play an important role in exercising global influence and in determining favourable policies for India in their countries of current residence.For example, Indian community based in United States has played an important role in the betterment of bilateral ties between India and America. People of Indian origin today occupy topmost political offices, cabinet ranks in many countries. Kamala Harris, Rishi Sunak, Priti Patel, Nikki Haley, Tulsi Gabbard are few such names. They have carved a niche for themselves , members of parliament in many countries.In the world of technology and business too they have carved a niche for themselves. The CEO's of companies like Google, Microsoft, IBM, Adobe, Vimeo, Starbucks etc. are people of Indian origin.

2. Cinema

Indian film industry produces the highest number of films per year. These movies have a global audience spread across the world specially in nations where Indian diaspora are based. Indian cinema has played important role in creating a positive and attractive image of India abroad. According to website statista.com the net value of Indian film industry in 2021was 183 Billion rupees(Basuroy, 2021) and it has been an important source of revenue and employment. In year 2017 totalrevenue earned by Indian movies from overseas market was $367 million (Vohra ,2018). Even the unexplored countries like China have emerged as new markets for Indian cinema. Movies of Aamir Khan like Dangal and Secret Superstar have been superhit blockbusters in China. These days many film festivals, functions, theme weddingscentred around Bollywood are being organised. Many prestigious international universities offer courses and research into this form of popular culture. The Indian film starsare recognised faces on the international advertising and entertainment media sphere.

3. Yoga & Spirituality

India has been seen as the land of yoga and spirituality for very long time. It gained a new momentum after the United Nations in 2014 proclaimed 21st June as the International Day of Yoga. The draft resolution proposed by India was supported by a recordnumber of 175 nations. According to website Yogaearth (2022) approximately 300 million people practise yoga regularly across the world out of which 36 million are in America alone. Worldwide yoga industry has been evaluated to be a $30 billion-plus business (Rowlatt,2015).Many forms of yoga and meditation taught by Indian gurus, yoga trainers and spiritual organizations have gained global mass following. acceptability. Indian spiritual organizations have their ashrams in different countries and have huge number of followers.Each year a larger number of foreigners flock to spiritual cities like Rishikesh, Haridwar, Mathura, Varanasi etc. India is also making a name for itself as a health and wellness destination offering yogic therapy, panch karma, naturopathy and as an ayurvedicretreat center.

4. Tourism

India offers a huge diversity in terms of experience to tourists in terms of different climatic and geographic locations (forests, rivers, mountains, deserts and beaches), Tiger reserves, Elephant corridors, National Parks, historical monuments and sites, religious, cultural and spiritual places. As of 2022 there are 40 UNESCO world heritage sites located in India. Various annual fairs and festivals organized in different parts of country add to the diverse colour of India. Very few countries in the world have this eclectic fusion of the traditional and the modern, the historical and the contemporary, the mountains and the seas, the deserts and the forests, and the different religions and communities. Buddha circuit, Ramayana circuit and Historical places are connected with special trains to boost tourism in the country. Besides these India is also fast emerging as a destination for medical tourism. It offers high quality treatment and healthcare services at an affordable price which is unimaginable in countries like US and UK.A positive national image leads to increase in tourism and this was the reason why Incredible India campaign was launched by Ministry of Tourism in 2002. The aim wasto promote India as a world-class tourist destination.The campaign proved to be successful, leading to a 16% increase in tourist traffic in its first year. The arrival of foreign tourists to India increased from 2.38 million in 2002 to 7.7 million in 2014 and in 2016 this number rose up to 8.80 million.

5. Cuisines

Indian cuisines which have a very wide range with each state having their own unique culinary dishes and flavours has gained global popularity. This can be understood by the fact that in Britain chicken tikka masala is the most popular dish and has become an integral part of British culture.Indic diaspora have been one of the key reasons behind the popularity of these cuisines. This diverse range includes Punjabi, Tamil, Mughlai, Rajasthani, Kashmiri, Malayali food etc. with hundreds ofvegetarian and non-vegetarian items. Restaurants serving Indian food can be found in almost all major cities of the world.Indian food is one of the most globalizedalong with Italian, Chinese and American fast food. A research paper published by US economist Joel Waldfogel in 2019in the *National Bureau of Economic Research* journal showed that Indian food was the fourth most popular in the entire world. It was especially popular in United Kingdom, South Korea, Thailand, Japan, Germany, France and US. According to Thussu (2013) the curry industry in Britain was worth 3.6 billion pounds annually with 10000 restaurants across the country employing 80000 people.

6. Culture

Cultural diplomacy has been an integral part of soft power diplomacy for a long time. Various aspects of Indian culture such as dance, music, theatre, visual arts, fairs, festivals, attire etc. has been a source of fascination and huge attraction for foreign nationals. It is in this very spirit that a dedicated organization called as Indian Council for Cultural Relations (ICCR) was started way back in 1950 to organize cultural festivals in India and abroad. As of 2022 the ICCR operates 38 Indian Cultural Centers across in various major cities of the world with the aim to spread Indian culture. Similarly, Society for the Promotion of Indian Classical Music And Culture Amongst Youth (SPIC MACAY) was started in 1977 as a voluntary youth movement to promote various aspects Indian culture such as Indian classical music, classical dance, folk music, yoga, meditation, crafts and other aspects of Indian culture.One more area related to culture that has garnered a lot of attention is Indian attire. The traditional clothes such as sarees, salwar suits,designer lehengas, hand embroidered dresses, khadi etc. have witnessed rising demands. Rise of e-commerce platforms, large Indian diaspora and the global influence of Bollywood are some of the reasons behind it.

7. **Civilization connect**

Indian civilization has also acted as a source of soft power since time immemorial. Countries based in South Asian subcontinent (Pakistan, Bangladesh, Bhutan, Sri Lanka etc.) have a deep imprint of this Indic culture.Indic cultural influence can also be observed in the Southeast Asian regions of Vietnam, Cambodia, Malay Peninsula, Sumatra, Java, Bali, Indonesia etc.some of which were parts of the Srivijaya kingdom in the eleventh century. Similarity can be noticed in the cultural practices, mythology,languages, scripts, written tradition, literatures, calendars, architectural styles, beliefs systems and art. For example, different versions of the ancient Indian epic Ramayana can be found in Southeast Asian nations. According to Malone (2011) Hinduism found its way across much of Indonesia, Malaysia and Thailand while Buddhism reached Japan and Vietnam through China and Korea and also flourished in countries closer to India such as Burma, Cambodia and Thailand.

Conclusion

From the discussions made in this paper, it can be concluded that India uses a variety of elements to spread soft power which mainly includes its diaspora, cinema, yoga, art & culture, music, cuisines, historical and civilizational links. These elements shape Indian foreign policy and its global image in a positive manner by increasing its global appeal and acceptability. French (2011) observed that in Western view until few years back India was all about "disease, dirt and deities" and it was assumed that that "it would always be like this". A nation which was "exotic, eternal, to be admired and patronized, but incapable of helping itself" dependent on the charity of outsiders and was not seen as a country that can ever "take off and revitalize itself". But India has proved its critics wrong.As declared by Prime Minister in his Independence Day speech this year India plans to become a developed country by 2047. Soft power diplomacy or cultural diplomacy has a great role to play in making India a global power.

References

French, P. (2011). *India: A Portrait*. Penguin.

Galloway, L. (2020). *Five superpowers ruling the world in 2050*. https://www.bbc.com/travel/article/20200322-five-superpowers-ruling-the-world-in-2050

Hall, I. (2012). India's New Public Diplomacy. *Asian Survey*, 52(6), 1089–1110. https://doi.org/10.1525/as.2012.52.6.1089

Isar, Y. R. (2017). Cultural diplomacy: India does it differently. *International Journal of Cultural Policy, 23*(6), 705–716. https://doi.org/10.1080/10286632.2017.1343310

Krishnakutty, P. (2021). All about International Solar Alliance, co-founded by France & India, to promote solar energy. *ThePrint.* https://theprint.in/theprint-essential/all-about-international-solar-alliance-co-founded-by-france-india-to-promote-solar-energy/594010/

Kugiel, P. (2012). India's Soft Power in South Asia. *International Studies, 49*(3–4), 351–376. https://doi.org/10.1177/0020881714534033

Luce, E. (2008). *In Spite of the Gods: The Rise of Modern India* (First). Anchor Books.

Lodhi, M. (2021, February 8). *Why a national image matters.* DAWN.COM. https://www.dawn.com/news/1606151

Machaiah, M. G. (2019, August 25). *Our country and its many hues* [News]. Deccan Herald. https://www.deccanherald.com/sunday-herald/sh-top-stories/our-country-and-its-many-hues-756342.html

Mahapatra, D. A. (2016). From a latent to a 'strong' soft power? The evolution of India's cultural diplomacy. *Palgrave Communications, 2*(1), 16091. https://doi.org/10.1057/palcomms.2016.91

Mazumdar, A. (2018). India's Soft Power Diplomacy Under the Modi Administration: Buddhism, Diaspora and Yoga.*Asian Affairs, 49*(3), 468–491. https://doi.org/10.1080/03068374.2018.1487696

Malone, D. M. (2011). *Does the Elephant Dance?* Oxford.

Miller, S. (2014). *A Strange Kind of Paradise: India through Foreign Eyes* (First). Penguin Books

Mukherjee,R. The False Promise of India's Soft Power. *Geopolitics, History, and International Relations* , Vol. 6, No. 1 (2014), pp. 46-62 Published by: Addleton Academic Publishers

Mukherjee, R., & Malone, D. M. (2011). From High Ground to High Table: The Evolution of Indian Multilateralism. *Global Governance, 17*(3), 311–329. https://www.jstor.org/stable/23033750

Pande, A. (2017). *From Chanakya To Modi: Evolution of India's Foreign Policy.* Harper Collins.

Pradhan, R., & Mohapatra, A. (2020). India's diaspora policy: evidence of soft power diplomacy under Modi. *South Asian Diaspora, 12*(2), 145–161. https://doi.org/10.1080/19438192.2020.1712792

PTI (2019) India lifted 271 million people out of poverty in 10 years: UN. *The Hindu.* https://www.thehindu.com/news/national/india-lifted-271-million-people-out-of-poverty-in-10-years-un/article28397694.ece

PTI. (2021). *India has supplied over 723 lakh doses of Covid vaccine to 94 countries, two UN entities: Govt.* The New Indian Express. https://www.newindianexpress.com/nation/2021/dec/07/india-has-supplied-over-723-lakh-doses-of-covid-vaccine-to-94-countries-two-un-entities-govt-2392832.html

Raghavan, S. (2018). *The Most Dangerous Place: A History of the United States in South Asia* (First). Penguin Random House India.

Rowlatt, J. (2015). Modi enlists yoga for "brand India." *BBC News.* https://www.bbc.com/news/world-asia-33214727

Shukla, S. (2019, August 29). Indian food fourth most popular in the world, a study of cuisine trade finds. *ThePrint.* https://theprint.in/world/indian-food-fourth-most-popular-in-the-world-a-study-of-cuisine-trade-finds/283119/

Tharoor, S. (2012). *Elephant; the Tiger & the Cellphone: Reflections on India in 21st Century.* Penguin Books India.

Thussu, D. K. (2013). *Communicating India's Soft Power: Buddha to Bollywood.* Palgrave Macmillan.

Thussu, D. K. (2016). The soft power of popular cinema – the case of India. *Journal of Political Power, 9*(3), 415–429. https://doi.org/10.1080/2158379X.2016.1232288

Vohra, P. (2018, August 3). *Indian movies attract millions around the world — and that number looks set to grow.* CNBC. https://www.cnbc.com/2018/08/03/indian-films-attract-millions-globally-and-it-appears-to-be-growing.html

Wang, J. (Ed.). (2011). *Soft Power in China: Public Diplomacy through Communication.* Palgrave Macmillan.

Wagner, C. (2010). India's Soft Power: Prospects and Limitations. *India Quarterly: A Journal of International Affairs, 66*(4), 333–342. https://doi.org/10.1177/097492841006600401

Yogaearth. (2022). 50 Blissful Yoga Statistics for 2022. *Yoga Earth.* https://yogaearth.com/yoga-research/yoga-statistics/

TEN

INTERNATIONAL DIPLOMACY VIA SOFT POWER: INDIA AND BHUTAN RELATIONS

Malsawmtluangi [1] and Prof. Nagalaxmi M Raman. [2]

[1]Research Scholar, Amity Institute of International Studies, Amity University Uttar Pradesh, Noida, India.

[2] Director & Head, Amity Institute of International Studies, Amity University Uttar Pradesh, Noida, India.

Abstract

India and Bhutan relations have been considered friendly since the 1950s. The relations between India and Bhutan were considered soft power due to the then Prime Minister Jawaharlal Nehru reaching out to Bhutan with an intention to form a special relationship and strengthen their relations as neighboring countries. In 1968, the diplomatic relations were strengthened with the establishment of a special office in Thimphu. The diplomatic relationship between the two countries can be traced back with the Treaty of Friendship and Cooperation signed by the two countries in 1949, since then India and Bhutan shared a unique and bilateral relationship, identified by its mutual understanding. A mutually beneficial project on Hydro-power relations with India and Bhutan is the core thread of the bilateral relationship between the two countries. This paper will focus on the trading process of India and Bhutan, since Bhutan's largest trading and business partner is India, focusing on the import and export since the signing of Treaty of Friendship in 1949 and the hydro-power relations.

Keywords: India and Bhutan relations, diplomacy, diplomatic relations, soft power, bilateral relationship, hydro-power relations, import and export, trading partner, business partner.

INTRODUCTION

After the independence, India has started cutting out its cultural ties to the other Asian region. India and Bhutan have shared a special relationship since the mid 1900's, it can be considered as a soft power when both the countries came together to form a healthy and good relationship to fulfill their national interests. India's soft power towards Bhutan can be seen in how India chose to form its foreign policies to culture from economic provinces. Nepal, Sikkim and Bhutan had formed a belt between the two superpowers India and China. The external and internal stability of these landlocked and small states depends heavily on the attitude of the two big countries from the north and south. The small neighbor countries' economic development also highly depends on the relationship with the two big superpower countries India and China. Bhutan expanded its territory over Cooch Bihar and some parts of Assam, that was when Bhutan came into contact with the British Colonial power in India. The contact of British India with Bhutan established the monarchy in Bhutan through the Wangchuk dynasty in 1907.[1] With the expansion of British involvement in India, the border of both the countries has become subsequent. Due to that, certain disputes and controversy happened between the two countries India and Bhutan, the Government of British India took this opportunity as creating a rival and controversy towards Bhutan, and this incident led to the war on Bhutan in the year 1864. The Government of British India has concluded the Treaty of 1910, which convicts the British under the possession of British India.[2] It is an important contribution to the study of India and Bhutan relations at the time when the Himalayas are growing in India and the world. With the expansion of the British Empire in India, the boundary of both countries became concurrent, the paper will not focus only on the states but analyzes their disputes and also the root causes of the issues. The war between Anglo-Bhutanese had a huge effect among both parties and the British Empire as well. The paper will focus on the various stages and causes of these phases of the relationship between India and Bhutan and how the British also played an important role in between the two countries. The soft power between India and Bhutan has been the main components of their on-going relationship.

RATIONALE OF THE STUDY

The main objective of the Government of British India was to strengthen India's traditional borders on the North region of Asia. he British national interest towards the Himalayan kingdom was shaped by the geopolitical aspects of the region_[3]. The main threats towards the northern border of India came from Russia. Nevertheless, the Anglo-Russian Convention of 1907 neutralized the main threat from Russia. China has always viewed the Himalayan region as 'part of her sphere'. After India got independence, there were doubts on whether India would honor the old treaties which served mostly the colonial national interest. It had become difficult for India to choose between the policy towards the anti-colonial record and its national interest. The Government of India made sure that whatever the countries the British had divided, India would arise from the obligations. Due to this reason, the government of India has to undertake various re-negotiation with some of the treaties he had signed with the other countries, including the Treaties with Bhutan. In the year 2946, Bhutan had visited India for consultation regarding the transfer of power and its future set-up on the development projects of the country. The treaty of friendship signed by India and Bhutan had an essence of British policy which safeguard the national interest of India in a certain important area. According to Article 2 of the Treaty of Friendship, the Government of India tackle to utilize any interference in the administration of Bhutan internally. The treaty which was signed in 1949 has become the main factors which maintained the bilateral relationship between India and Bhutan. On the other hand, the government of Bhutan had also agreed on taking the guidance and advice of the government of India in terms of her external relationship and administration. The government of India after having an effective role in controlling the external administration of Bhutan, India had established its protectorate over Sikkim, India desired to exclude all the foreign intrigues and influence from this area. India has claimed that she will be responsible for protecting the borders of Sikkim and Bhutan, and its integrity between the two states and to maintain peace and prosperity on any aggression between the two countries Sikkim and Bhutan_[4] In the meantime, China has also tried its best on influencing Himalayan region with an intention of expanding and spreading in the area. This highly depends on the degree of the political leaders among the border states appraising China's intentions and motivation. Despite the constant influence of Chinese propaganda amongst Bhutan, Bhutan and India still remain intact on their friendship and good intentions towards each other, and serve each other's national interest, this has proved the foundation of the relationship between India and Bhutan, and the strong bond they have between each other. India and Bhutan have a trouble-free relationship compared to the relationship between the countries in the South Asian region, India and Bhutan shared a bilateral relationship where they have a deep connection amongst each other on the basis of cultures, traditional ties, warm and friendly close link. The majority of the development in Bhutan is either guided or funded by the Government of India, the Government of Bhutan launched the 'Operations All Clear' under the pressure of India to clear out the Indian militants on the year 2003, where the Bhutanese military was aided by the Government of India, however, this operation ended in 2004. Nevertheless, India is accountable for Bhutanese economic development and Bhutanese Security, Indian Military Training Team (IMTRAT) was established to provide training to the squad of Bhutanese Security Forces.[5] By any means possible, Bhutan economy is entirely dependent upon Indian funds. This project was initiated by Nehru, who initiated Bhutan economic development. As one of the least developed countries, Bhutan is solely dependent upon foreign aid for its economic development and programmers. Mutual understanding and linkage between India and Bhutan have benefited both the countries national interest, this has become the main elements for their bilateral relationship. The first five-year plan was launched in the 1960's and this has been the main financial assistance for Bhutan's economic development. So far as per the analysis, nine Five Year Plan (FYP) has been completed. Majority of the districts in Bhutan are attainable by road, funded and constructed utterly by the Government of India; Indian Border Road Organization (BRO) The famous Hydropower projects in Bhutan are also funded by the Government of India, which contain three Hydropower projects, roads construction projects, Paro airport projects, cement plants and Electricity distribution and transmission system. The relationship between India and Bhutan is conceivably the only bilateral relationship in South Asia, which possesses the high excess to both the countries. On the one hand, Bhutan had accepted India as its economic assistance, on the other hand India tends to become sensitive when it comes to Bhutan's developmental requirement. This has created a unique relationship between the two countries which made Bhutan shaped a developmental trajectory solely based on the gross national happiness. Over the past few years, this bilateral relationship has become a partnership in a comprehensive manner with a wide range of issues. Nevertheless, hydropower and infrastructure were the main reasons with Indian government authority to visit Bhutan, during the King Wangchuk visit in India in 2008, 12 memorandums of understanding (MOU) were signed between India and Bhutan on certain issues like cooperation on environmental related issues, technical cooperation, agriculture research, information technology, civil aviation, prevention of trafficking of narcotic drugs and health issues. The energy sector of four hydropower projects was the top priority on their agreement. India had also assured that Bhutan will get help and guidance from India regarding its National Transmission Grid master plan.

OBJECTIVES

- To allude to the role of India in Bhutan's international affairs.
- To gain familiarity with the role of soft power in the international diplomacy between India and Bhutan.
- To comprehend the root causes of the border issues between Bhutan and China.
- To evaluate the factors taken by India to support Bhutan's economic development.

RESEARCH QUESTIONS

The research questions are concerned with the international diplomacy via soft power which takes place between India and Bhutan relations.

- What is the role of India in advancing Bhutan's economic development?
- How does China intervene in India and Bhutan relationship?
- How does the Indian Government assist Bhutan in expanding its foreign affairs?

RESEARCH METHODOLOGY

To recap, the aim of this paper is to analyze, describe and examine the international diplomacy via soft power with concern to India and Bhutan relationship. This study provides us with:

- The role of India in Bhutan internal and external affairs.
- The measures taken by China to interrupt India and Bhutan relations.

The research methodology focuses on the research questions, the objectives and the aims of this research paper. These are the different methods used to analyze the data:

- Analytical analysis. (Articles, Journals, Research Paper and Books)
- Case study analysis. (Articles, Journals, Research Paper and Books)
- Descriptive analysis. (Articles, Journals, Research Paper and Books)

In order to analyze the research paper, qualitative research methodology is carried out to perceive analytical analysis, Case study analysis and descriptive analysis.

ANALYSIS AND FINDINGS

- Up until 1959, Bhutan had followed the policy of isolationism, on the year 1971, February 7, the United Nations Security Council had voted Bhutan to be the 128th member nation. In that year, the India Prime Minister Nehru had visited Bhutan and King Jigme Dorji Wangchuk and Nehru came to the conclusion that national progress cannot be achieved with limited international intercourse, the Bhutanese authorities had begun negotiating with the Indian Planning Commission for the Five Year Development Plan. Economic development for the Kingdom of Bhutan had become the foremost topic for the two day discussion on September 26, 1958, where Nehru focused on the road development between India and Bhutan, and inside Bhutan itself. Nehru also emphasized on the willingness of India to assist Bhutan on technical aid and any kinds of assistance. The first five year plan which lasted from 1961-1966 was entirely financed by India, the total expenditure was estimated to be around 101.2 million rupees. Moreover, India had aided 300 million rupees to Bhutan for road constructions by the Indian Border Roads Organization. The second five year plan which lasted from 1966 to 1971, the total estimated expenditure was 200 million rupees, which was also financed by India. The main focus during this plan was education, agriculture, public works and health.[6] A third five year plan was introduced to be more focused on the small cottage industries with an acknowledgment on education, agriculture and public health with providing aid to the Bhutan countries. In the beginning of the first five year plan, a department of health care facilities was built for the first time within the Government of Bhutan. As the Indian government informed Bhutan on its vast natural resources within the Government of Bhutan, henceforth Bhutan government has immense control over forest reserves and geological surveys. The foundation of the relationship between India and Bhutan was based on the Treaty of Friendship signed on August 8, 1949, this treaty was an edited version of the Sinchula Treaty which was signed on November 11, 1865, by British India and the Maharaja of Bhutan. The economic development of Bhutan is highly dependent on the fund and the guidance of India into certain aspects. India and Bhutan have unique bilateral relationships in the South Asia region and their good relationship has protected the both countries from external threats.

- According to Bhutan, China has been trying to build a road across Doklam with an intention of extending its territory. Doklam is located near Yadongog Tibetan region and the Ha Valley of Bhutan. Doklam has been declared disputed by both the countries China and Bhutan. Doklam region is specifically concluded in India's sovereign territory. Even though diplomatic relations were not visible to the eye, there have been several border disputes between China and Bhutan, which resulted in signing the agreement in 1984 by Bhutan and China regarding the solving of border issues. Nevertheless, according to Bhutan, China has been violating the agreement since 1988 by attempting to construct roads, and the same happened in the year 1998, in an attempt to expand its project on 'One Belt One Road Project'. Many have argued that the actions was not considered to be border disputes, but some had also argued that even though the intention was merely on constructing roads, this action can also leads to making the 'Chinese Dream' come true, their hidden objectives on making this plan succeed can be one of the many reasons why China tends to disrespect their border agreement with Bhutan._[7]

- Despite the Chinese provocation and propaganda with Bhutan, India and Bhutan are still having the most friendly bilateral relations_[8] Bhutan always supported India when it came to SAARC forums, as its closest ally in the South Asian region. According to the Article 2 of the Treaty of Friendship signed by India and Bhutan, Bhutan agreed on taking the advice and the guidance from India when it comes to dealing with external and international affairs, similarly, India also agreed on helping and guiding Bhutan at whatever help is needed, this also become relevant on helping its internal affairs, where Indian Government funded and aided most of the economic development by Bhutan. India also supported Bhutan when it came to involvement in external or international organization. In April 2010, India gave full support to Bhutan hosting the SAARC Summit. India encouraged Bhutan to be more invested in the international organization for forming allies and have a better understanding of other countries from different perspectives.

CONCLUSION

To conclude this paper, I would like to highlight the importance of India to the Government of Bhutan. The economic development in Bhutan is entirely funded and assisted by India. The Free Trade Agreement was signed in the year 2006, Bhutan only utilized 30 percent of its power generated, while the remaining was sold to India, which makes it one of the most exported by Bhutan. The main economic development project between India and Bhutan is the four hydropower projects, these projects have helped India and Bhutan at the same time. India had assured Bhutan that these plans will help Bhutan on its National Transmission Grid master plan. Despite China constantly on a mission of expanding its territory by constructing roads through Doklami.e under the region of Bhutan, Bhutan chose to stay loyal to India and this bilateral relationship has resulted in both the countries having their national interest supplied. India had supported Bhutan on any of its international diplomacy with other countries or organizations, this has helped in boosting their friendship and India had encouraged Bhutan to start forming international companions to gain allies. Therefore, the international diplomacy between India and Bhutan via soft power had bestowed benefits to both the countries.

REFERENCES

- Das, Suranjan and Chakrabarti,Shantanu, (2007) **"India and Bhutan: The Case of a Symbiotic Relationship?"**, India's Foreign Affairs Journal, vol.2, No.3, Jul-sep., 2007, Pp73-90.
- K. Mitra, Subrata and Thaliyakkattil, (2018) "Bhutan and Sino–Indian Rivalry: The Price of Proximity", University of California Press, vol. 58, No. 2, March-April, 2018, Pp- 240-260.
- J. Belfiglio, Valentine, (1972) **"India's Economic and Political Relations with Bhutan"**, University of California Press, vol. 12, No. 8, August, 1972, pp 676-685.
- Mathur, A. (1974). *Reviewed Work:* **"INDIA AND BHUTAN by KapileshwarLabh."** India Quarterly by Sage Publications, Inc, vol. 30, no. 4, oct- dec 1974, pp 336-337.
- Poulose, T. T. (1971, April). **"Bhutan's External Relations and India"** Cambridge University Press. Vol. 20, No. 2 Apr., 1971, pp. 195-212.

- Lok Sabha Debates (1959), Second Series , vol. 33. Cols 4800-4801.
- Sarkar, T. (2022, April-June). **"INDIA - BHUTAN RELATIONS"**Indian Political Science Association. Vol. 73, No. 2, April-June, 2022, pp. 347-352.
- Haran, V. P. (2017, Aug 1).**" BHUTAN"** Institute of Peace and Conflict Studies. From the report "3 Years of the Modi Government". pp. 41-43.
- Sharma, Harvir. (1994, June-September). **"BHUTAN AND ITS REGIONAL SECURITY ENVIRONMENT"** Sage Publications, Inc. Vol. 50, No. 3, pp. 25-42 (18 pages).
- Joseph C., M. (2007, January-March). **"India-Bhutan Relations: An Overview"**. Prints Publications Pvt Ltd. Vol. 2, No. 1, pp. 88-101.
- Karan P.K (1963) "Geopolitical Structure of Bhutan" India Quarterly, PP-203-213.
- Choudhary, L. K. (2005, April-June). **"Indo-Bhutan Relationship: A Unique Example of Bilateral Friendship in South Asia"**Sage Publications, Inc. Vol. 61, No. 2, pp. 213-229.
- A. Andelman, D. (2010, March- June). **"Bhutan, Borders, and Bliss"** Duke University Press. Vol. 27, No. 1, pp. 103-111.
- P. Karan, Pradyumna. (1963, July-September). **'GEOPOLITICAL STRUCTURE OF BHUTAN'** Sage Publications, Inc. Vol. 19, No. 3, pp.203-213.
- Kohli, M. (1986, April-June). **"BHUTAN'S STRATEGIC ENVIRONMENT: CHANGING PERCEPTIONS."** Sage Publications, Inc. Vol.42, No. 2, pp 142- 153.
- S. Kharat, R. (2001, January-March). **"THE ETHNIC CRISIS IN BHUTAN : ITS IMPLICATIONS"** Sage Publications, Inc. Vol. 57, No. 1 pp 39-50.
- Bisht, M. (2014, March 1). **"An Agenda for the New Government on JSTOR"** Institute of Peace and Conflict Studies. Issue Brief-248, pp1-8.
- Pandey, S. (1982, April-June). **"MINI-MAXI PARTNERS A LOOK AT INDIA-BHUTAN RELATIONS"**. Indian Political Science Association. Vol. 43, No. 2, pp. 86-106.
- Mathou, T. (2018, January-February). **"Bhutan in 2017: Preparing a New Cycle"** University of California Press. Vol. 58, No. 1
- The Europe Year Book, 1871, Vol II, Europa Publications Limited, London, p. 100.
- Jha, T. (2013, August). **"China and its Peripheries: Limited Objectives in Bhutan."** Institute of Peace and Conflict Studies. Issue Brief 233, pp 1-8.
- Sherpa, S. (2013-2014, November-February). **"Bhutan: Between Two Giants"** Duke University Press. Vol.30, No.4, pp-41-44.

- Rajput, M. (2014, January-March). **"INDO-BHUTAN RELATIONS: A CRITICAL ANALYSIS"** Indian Political Science Association. Vol. 75, No. 1, pp-149-156.
- Sarki, A. (2019, October). *India–Bhutan Relations:* **"PARADIPLOMACY, DOMESTIC CONSIDERATIONS AND NEW DELHI'S PREROGATIVE"**Kapur Surya Foundation. Vol. 23,No. 4, pp. 138-151.
- BadrulBeena, M. (2019, January- March). **"The Doklam Stalemate: THE TRI-JUNCTION BETWEEN BHUTAN, CHINA AND INDIA"**Kapur Surya Foundation. Vol.23, No. 1, pp. 60-69
- Mathou, T. (2017, January-February). **"Bhutan in 2016: A New Era Is Born"** University of California Press. Vol. 57, No. 1, pp- 56-59.
- Kumar Mishra, M. (2020, July-September). **"India In The Himalayan Landscape: SECURITY CONCERNS AND APPROACHES"**Kapur Surya Foundation. Vol. 24, No. 3, pp- 20-41.
- Muni, S. D. (1991, September). **"Bhutan in the Throes of Ethnic Conflict"** India International Centre. Vol. 18, No. 1, pp-145-154.

[1]_Das, Suranjan and Chakrabarti,Shantanu, (2007) **"India and Bhutan: The Case of a Symbiotic Relationship?"**, India's Foreign Affairs Journal, vol.2, No.3, Jul-sep., 2007, Pp73-90.

[2]_Mathur, A. (1974). *Reviewed Work:* **"INDIA AND BHUTAN by KapileshwarLabh."** India Quarterly by Sage Publications, Inc, vol. 30, no. 4, oct- dec 1974, pp 336-337.

[3]_ Karan P.K (1963) "Geopolitical Structure of Bhutan" India Quarterly, PP-203-213.

[4]_ Lok Sabha Debates (1959), Second Series , vol. 33. Cols 4800-4801.

[5]_Sarkar, T. (2022, April-June). **"INDIA - BHUTAN RELATIONS"**Indian Political Science Association. Vol. 73, No. 2, April-June, 2022, pp. 347-352.

[6]_The Europe Year Book, 1871, Vol II, Europa Publications Limited, London, p. 100.

[7]_BADRUL BEENA, M. (2019, January). *The Doklam Stalemate: THE TRI-JUNCTION BETWEEN BHUTAN, CHINA AND INDIA.* World Affairs: The Journal of International Issues.

[8]_Poulose, T. T. (1971, April). **"Bhutan's External Relations and India"** Cambridge University Press. Vol. 20, No. 2 Apr., 1971, pp. 195-212.

ELEVEN

DIGITAL DIPLOMACY THROUGH SOCIAL MEDIA: BENEFITS, ISSUES AND THREATS

Lohita Raulo

Research Scholar

Department of Mass Communication & Journalism

Tezpur University, Assam, India

Email- Raulolohita15@gmail.com

Uttam Kr Pegu

Professor

Department of Mass Communication

Rajiv Gandhi University, Rono Hills, Arunachal Pradesh, India

Email-Kp.uttam@gmail.com

Abstract

International relations are indispensable in fostering good relations with other countries in the era of globalization; diplomacy has always been a crucial component of them. In this technological age, social media is one of the simpler ways to connect with other nations. There is a literature gap in investigating India's mediated diplomacy on social media and how social media as a medium has fostered ties and agenda building with different nations. The study aims to justify and gauge social media as an effective and important tool for fostering international relations. Twitter has developed into forums for direct communication between the Indian policy establishment and its domestic and international constituents. This study explores how digital communication has impacted India's standing abroad by outlining the essential traits of Indian digital communication and assessing its efficacy and how the media landscape has transformed as a result of the rapid growth of technology, and new challenges have emerged for the digital diplomacy institutions. The study undertakes a qualitative assessment of social media accounts of Ministry of External Affairs on Twitter. The results highlight vital benefits such as real-time reach on key pressing issues, and expanded engagements that further aid the diplomacy objectives laid by India. A key challenge identified was navigating the array of information in the age of misinformation and information overload. The advantages and disadvantages of using social media suggest that it's an important medium to convey information to the citizens and to other countries.

Introduction

The two components of foreign policy are the methods and the goals that must be accomplished on a national level. The relationship between national objectives and the resources needed to achieve them is a recurring theme in statecraft. The means of achieving a nation's foreign policy goals is thus one of the components of foreign policy, and diplomacy is one of the main tools of foreign policy (Adesina, 2017). A type of contemporary public diplomacy known as "digital diplomacy" combines social media, new information and communication technologies (ICT), and the internet to improve diplomatic ties. Greater access to information, more contact between people and organizations, and greater transparency are the primary differences from traditional public diplomacy (Chakraborty, 2013). It is now common for ministries, embassies, and representatives of international organizations to update their websites. The websites of foreign ministries serve to describe and document their country's foreign policies and refute objectionable acts or assertions made by other states (Barston, 2014). Social media have developed into additional crucial diplomatic instruments.

Although exchanges between officials of sovereign governments, the traditional form of conducting diplomacy, remain essential, individuals and organizations—rather than just countries—play a more significant role in international affairs today because of how linked the world is. As a result, there is now a field known as "digital diplomacy" (Stanzel et al., 2018).

Digital diplomacy has recently attracted researchers' attention in mass communication, peace and conflict studies, and international affairs. Because of social media and modern technology, governments, individuals, and organizations now have more ways than ever to interact with overseas audiences. According to the literature on digital diplomacy, social media can aid nations in enhancing their goodwill through involvement and communication (Iteefaq, 2019). According to Gilboa, "social media platforms like Facebook, Twitter, and YouTube are new instruments for promoting engagement with audiences in a developing information environment. They have not fundamentally transformed the aims of public diplomacy.

Kampf et al. (2015) claim that digital diplomacy primarily refers to a nation's expanding use of social media platforms to further its foreign policy objectives and actively manage its image and reputation. They pointed out that there are two levels of digital diplomacy: the foreign ministry and the embassies spread out over the globe. By working on these two levels, states can adapt their nation-branding and foreign policy communications to local audiences' distinct histories, cultures, values, and traditions, promoting their desired image and fostering acceptance of their foreign policy.

Digital Diplomacy and Social Media

World leaders and diplomats speak and interact with the public they want to influence directly through social media, mainly Twitter. Internet tools are also being used more to support diplomatic activities. Governments might view the Internet as a unique diplomatic tool; through its proper use, they can "advertise" not just their positions on various problems but also promote their ideas globally. If performed well, such a role aids in the embassy's image-building efforts in the host state, which benefits the state it represents.

Bjola & Jiang (2015) propound three benefits of social media in public diplomacy: the efficiency of information distribution, the target audience reached, and a possibility for two-way contact between diplomats and the international audience.

Social media platforms have become essential to international leaders and diplomats. Despite being a little formal, practically everyone prefers Twitter as their social media platform. Twitter allows leaders to interact and establish direct connections with the audience they want to sway. Technology is evolving, and social media sites are getting significant updates virtually every other day (Martin et al., 2013). Social media has dramatically changed communication over the years, from straightforward texting to live broadcasting an event. With these developments, digital diplomacy has also changed to fit the times. Digital diplomacy aims to engage and persuade sizable populations in a short amount of time at a low cost of engagement (Khan et al., 2021). While it is undeniable that traditional diplomatic techniques continue to guide interactions regarding both domestic and foreign policy, there has been a striking increase in how governments are using technology as a new channel for communication to uphold their traditions and values both at home and abroad.

India's Digital Diplomacy

The MEA's digital diplomacy effort has done a fantastic job of both forming the foreign policy and creating a powerful and effective network with the populace, particularly the diaspora. Connecting with the Indian diaspora, which is widespread and huge, is essential to India's foreign policy. Regardless of what the policy stands for, it is always directly related to the diaspora. Policymakers and diplomats make it a point to include members of the Indian Diaspora in these discussions and debates (Garud-Patkar,2022).

India is one of the most active nations online; tweeting 43.1 times on average per month, and it has the most followers on diplomatic accounts (about 72.5 million as of June 2021). Being the first developing nation and BRICS member in terms of digital practises, India stands out in the realm of digital diplomacy. India has assumed a significant role on the global diplomatic stage since the establishment of a Public Diplomacy Division by the government in 2006 and the creation of social media profiles for its ministries and embassies. Social media has helped the nation become more powerful and has allowed it to grow its diplomatic network.

For instance, its Ministry of External Affairs recently surpassed 2.1 million followers on both its Facebook and Twitter sites, coming in second place to the U.S. Department of State, which amasses 2.3 million followers on its official Facebook page. This active digital diplomacy has been particularly useful in interacting with the populace, particularly the youth and the various strata of society, as well as with the 18 million-strong Indian diaspora, in addition to being used to promote the Indian foreign policy. As the nation continues to grow and acquire more worldwide influence, its digital diplomacy also continues to advance quickly, making India the nation that gains the most new followers each month (around 801k as of June 2021).

The digital entry of India into social media was made by @IndianDiplomacy with a tweet in July 2010; the account was primarily created to foster greater public diplomacy knowledge and engagement with the general population. 2011 saw the creation of the official @MEAIndia twitter account following its enormous success. Both Twitter accounts are owned by the Ministry of External Affairs, however they often serve different purposes. The Ministry of External Affairs' spokesperson's official Twitter handle is @MEAIndia, and it is this account's job to disseminate any formal announcement and remarks that the MEA has made in the public interest.

In 2011, as protests broke out in Libya and Egypt, the Indian foreign secretary Nirupama Rao used Twitter to organize the evacuation of Indian citizens from those nations. When someone contacted her, she would then dispatch directions on how to leave the crisis-hit area when tweeted her for assistance; Rao's method of immediately responding to inquiries about Indian foreign policy was "a prospect almost unheard of in India's bloated bureaucracy," according to Singh (2018).

The Indian government realized that social media must be used for all administrative tasks. The proposal, however, prompted questions about who has the authority to speak for the government and how much interaction the public should have with social media accounts (Pandey, 2013). The Indian government published an official draught of framework and guidelines that "the purpose behind the use of social media is not only to disseminate information but also to undertake a public engagement for a meaningful public participation in the formulation of public policy" (Pandey, 2013). This addressed these issues and encouraged agencies to use social media.

The 2014 general election was a turning point in Indian politics as most of the election campaigning was conducted online. Of all the candidates, the BJP specifically received social media support from millions of Indian youth. Through social media campaigns with attractive slogans, Narendra Modi engaged with the public in real-time. He broadcast his lectures on a YouTube channel and used WhatsApp messaging to invite supporters to his rallies. Additionally, he ran pages like "I support Narendra Modi," which received 12 million Facebook likes and 8 million Twitter likes. His rise to the second-most followed politician in the world on Twitter before the elections was evidence of the efficacy of his branding strategies.

Indian nationals caught up in far-off crises are increasingly receiving greater high-level attention regarding humanitarian issues. There has been a heightened sensitivity to public opinion when evaluating and reacting to such events. Consular and passport services have been delivered with notable improvements thanks to digital interactions.

Rationale of the study

According to a study by Ittefaq (2019), digital diplomacy in India is more structured and well-organized. India's digital diplomacy division and foreign office are more proactive than other public bodies in that country in terms of departmental usage of social media.

Recent research' contradicting findings call for further investigation into the interaction and communication between governmental organizations and "netizens" on social networking sites (SNS). The Digitalization of Public Diplomacy, a recent publication, used more than 90 items to gauge digital diplomacy. Few scholars have focused on developing countries' efforts in digital diplomacy with netizens to interact with them through live Q&A sessions, even though many studies have been conducted in the past ten years on the role of social media in public diplomacy concerning engagement and dialogue. Despite a gap in the literature on digital diplomacy, this study aims to examine how institutional Twitter accounts for Indian government officials use social media.

Research Objectives

The main objectives of this paper are

- To gauge the benefits and risks of digital diplomacy
- To assess the current trends of digital diplomacy with a focus on its content

Research Methodology

A quantitative content analysis of the Indian government accounts' Facebook and Twitter posts, namely those managed by the Indian Ministry of External Affairs. This study analyses the two twitter account @MEAIndia and @Indiandiplomacy.

According to Krippendorf (2013), content analysis is a technique for drawing conclusions about the context of usage from content (such as text, images, music, and art). The optimum method for this study is content analysis since it enables structured and impartial treatment of vast amounts of user-generated material. Content analysis is a suitable way to study tweets and status updates that the Indian government accounts share and publish on social media because Twitter generates a vast volume of data each day.

A total of n=165 tweets were collected from both the accounts utilizing a set of Twitter software protocols that enable for data extraction via any software application; this study was conducted using MAXQDA. Data were gathered from Twitter. It can access a user's profile to get access to a lot of metadata, including the user's followers, tweets, and profile pictures, among other things. The entire set of data was gathered between September 21 and September 30, 2022.Since, the data extraction from Twitter is limited to the previous 10 days.

The following standards were followed by the study for grouping tweets and status updates into a sampling frame:

- All tweets and status updates, with the exception of videos, are taken into account.
- Regardless of the interactive elements, a single tweet or status update that contains numerous interactive elements, such as photographs, gifs, or videos, is treated as a single unit.
- Only English-language posts are taken into consideration.
- Repeated tweets and status updates are removed.

Analysis and Findings

The @Indiandiplomacy account was created to promote public diplomacy-related awareness and communication with the public. 2011 saw the creation of the formal @MEAIndia twitter account following its tremendous success. Both Twitter accounts are owned by the Ministry of External Affairs, however they often have distinct functions. The Ministry of External Affairs' spokesperson's twitter Page account is @MEAIndia, and it is this account's job to disseminate any formal announcement and remarks that the MEA has made in the interest of the public. The Prime Minister's interactions with other heads of state, as well as state visits and appearances by the President, Vice President, External Affairs Minister, Minister(s) of State, and other senior foreign service officials, are all documented in photographs, clips, news releases.

Whereas, @IndianDiplomacy serves the purpose of promoting narratives pertain to culture and that of nation branding. This account captures the with a primary focus on Indian culture and tradition, narratives of Indian successes and positive stories from all over the planet, incredible information and facts regarding India expressing its rich and glorious heritage, public reports, mutual statements, and the appointment scheduling of new diplomats and ambassadors, it perfectly highlights the essence of soft diplomacy.

The analyses of the tweets are represented in a word cloud. The main focus of all the tweets are shown visually in a "word cloud." The word appears larger in the graphic created the more frequently the keyword occurs in the text being analyzed. Word clouds are being used more frequently as a quick method to determine the main idea of written content. They have been used, for instance, to visualize the content of political speeches in politics, business, and education.

Figure 1: Word Cloud of frequently appearing words

The word cloud in Figure 1 shows that 'India' is the most highlighted word in both twitter's handles. When analyzed with the general notion of the agenda set by the Indian Government, the word cloud clearly highlights that 'India' and 'PM' are the two most prominent and frequently appearing words with a frequency of 279 and 131 times, respectively. Most of the words in the word cloud resonate well with the current affairs and the aims of the Indian Government.

Notably, the most popular hashtags have been #Azaadikaamritmahotsav and #amritmahotsav used in more than 75 tweets separately. As India observes its 75th year of independence, the Prime Minister of India launched the campaign, emphasizing that India has undergone a dramatic transformation. This year of independence and the campaign focuses on respect for oneself and self-reliance. This was reflected in the tweets by the MEA's Twitter handle. The main goal of MEA is to promote Indian ideals worldwide while also building awareness of the nation through India's rich heritage, culture, and customs. MEA India is dedicated to attaining its objectives while utilizing contemporary connecting and communication technologies and keeping up with the rapidly evolving state of science and technology.

Benefits of Digital Diplomacy

1. *Strengthening International relations*

There are numerous forms and sizes of diplomacy. It is governed by presidents, prime ministers, attorneys, economists, scientists, humanitarians, and ambassadors. They exemplified both the multiplicity of prospective diplomatic actors and the consistency of what we might call the "diplomatic style" – the attempt to increase power and influence through creative alliances and techniques as opposed to blatant unilateral acts of force (Hutchings & Suri, 2015).

Foreign policy perspectives are being communicated to a broader cross-section of Indian society by leveraging the significant popular appeal of political leaders in ways never before thought possible. India's diplomatic outreach benefits greatly from Prime Minister Narendra Modi's widespread appeal on so many social media platforms. PM Modi's "Twiplomacy" is what public relations specialists dream of, from popularising the International Day of Yoga as a form of cultural diplomacy to inviting President Barack Obama to India's Republic Day celebrations in 2015 and receiving his answer on Twitter (Hindustan Times, 2021).

1. *Timeliness*

In many situations, having quick awareness of different events can help advance the national interest. Digital technologies are beneficial for quickly communicating in urgent situations and acquiring and analyzing information about the diplomatic activity. They make it possible for governments to consider how developments in other regions of the world may influence their nation. The definitions of long-standing techniques adopted by Indian diplomats, such as "quiet" diplomacy, "low-key" attempts, "considered" responses, and "discreet" inquiries, need to be recalibrated for use on digital platforms.

3. *Economically viable*

By encouraging public, media, and political-diplomatic interaction to bring about constructive change, Twitter messages can assist in investigating and identifying problematic issues and exposing those responsible. Due to its economic viability, digital diplomacy is more reasonable to governments, MFAs, and embassies to expand their work (Rashica, 2018).

4. *Increased Engagements*

The rise and deepening of political, economic, and cultural connections outside national borders characterize the globalization era. Digital diplomacy does not take the role of conventional diplomacy but can swiftly and more effectively bolster the state's efforts in international relations. It is now a crucial component for carrying out foreign policy. In order to further its foreign policy objectives, increase international alignment, and influence people who have never visited any of the world's embassies, digital diplomacy is quite helpful. Countries employ social media and digital diplomacy to preserve legitimacy and foster or bolster connections in a changing environment due to direct public participation and the involvement of non-state actors (Danziger & Schreiber,2021).

Risk of Digital Diplomacy

1. *Hacking*

A concern that has persisted since the creation of the Internet is hacking. A case in point is the suspected hacking of Syed Akbaruddin, India's permanent representative to the UN, by Turkish hackers in 2018. World leaders and diplomats are more vulnerable to cyberattacks as a result of their greater use of digital technologies. These dangers are posed by actors that want to obstruct communications and steal critical data for their purposes (The Wire, 2018).

2. *Misinformation*

The idea that social media, supported by algorithmic monitoring, is weakening varied online exchanges and conversation and, instead, is encouraging hyperpartisanship, political polarisation, and extreme online views is another subject of concern for diplomats. As a result, an audience is less inclined to engage in conversation or interaction with ambassadors, weakening the development of connections. Furthermore, widespread falsehoods weaken reality and the truth while diminishing the credibility of diplomatic organizations, which suffer collateral damage due to growing public suspicion (Antwi-Boateng, & Al Mazrouei, 2021). Additionally, media outlets deliberately misinform the public and taint the media's credibility as the fourth estate regarding democracy. As a result, ambassadors are forced to play media judges for the general public by advising them on which media sources are reliable and which are not.

Conclusion

Today's global community has undoubtedly changed due to the Internet, mainly social media. It has changed how diplomacy is conducted and has emerged as an undisputed avenue for diplomatic communication. Diplomats' use of social media has facilitated interaction between the public and decision-makers. These resources, particularly Facebook and Twitter, give foreign operations access to the people living inside and outside their own nations. Bypassing state and media censorship, this communication frequently gives nations the chance to influence global audiences and pursue diplomatic goals more successfully. Digital diplomacy thus presents both potential and difficulties. On the one side, excessive use of social media gives nations more information to address issues.

On the other hand, depending too much on social media as a diplomatic instrument has a variety of hazards. However, it seems that the opportunities outweigh the difficulties. The dissemination of a state's foreign policy positions to domestic and international audiences can be considerably aided by digital diplomacy and Internet-related operations.

Bibliography

Adesina, O. S. (2017). Foreign policy in an era of digital diplomacy. *Cogent Social Sciences*, *3*(1), 1297175.

Antwi-Boateng, O., & Al Mazrouei, K. A. M. (2021). The Challenges of Digital Diplomacy in the Era of Globalization: The Case of the United Arab Emirates. *International Journal of Communication, 15*, 19.

Barston, R. P. (2014). Modern diplomacy/RP Barston.

Bjola, C., & Jiang, L. (2015). Social media and public diplomacy: A comparative analysis of the digital diplomatic strategies of the EU, US and Japan in China. In *Digital Diplomacy* (pp. 71-88). Routledge.

Chakraborty, K. (2013). Cultural diplomacy dictionary. *Berlin: Academy for Cultural Diplomacy*, 36-37.

Danziger, R., & Schreiber, M. (2021). Digital diplomacy: Face management in MFA Twitter accounts. *Policy & Internet, 13*(4), 586-605.

Garud-Patkar, N. (2022). Is digital diplomacy an effective foreign policy tool? Evaluating India's digital diplomacy through agenda-building in South Asia. *Place Branding and Public Diplomacy, 18*(2), 128-143.

Gilboa, E. (2016). Digital diplomacy. *The SAGE handbook of diplomacy*, 540-551.

Hutchings, R., & Suri, J. (Eds.). (2019). *Modern diplomacy in practice.* Springer Nature.

Ittefaq, M. (2019). Digital diplomacy via social networks: A cross-national analysis of governmental usage of Facebook and Twitter for digital engagement. *Journal of Contemporary Eastern Asia, 18*(1), 49-69.

Kampf, R., Manor, I., & Segev, E. (2015). Digital diplomacy 2.0? A cross-national comparison of public engagement in Facebook and Twitter. *The Hague Journal of Diplomacy, 10*(4), 331-362.

Kent, M. L., & Taylor, M. (1998). Building dialogic relationships through the World Wide Web. Public relations review, 24(3), 321-334.

Khan, M. L., Ittefaq, M., Pantoja, Y. I. M., Raziq, M. M., & Malik, A. (2021). Public engagement model to analyze digital diplomacy on Twitter: A social media analytics framework. *International Journal of Communication, 15*, 29.

Krippendorff, K. (2013). Content analysis: An introduction to its methodology. Thousand Oaks, California: Sage.

Manor, I., & Segev, E. (2015). America's selfie: How the US portrays itself on its social media accounts. In *Digital diplomacy* (pp. 89-108). Routledge.

Martin, C., Jagla, L., & Firestone, C. M. (2013). Integrating diplomacy and social media. *Washington: Aspen Institute.*

Pandey, A. (2013, April 23). Social media governance in India. Retrieved from http://www.legalservicesindia.com/article/article/social-media-governance-inindia-1513-1.html

Rashica, V. (2018). The benefits and risks of digital diplomacy. *Seeu Review*, *13*(1), 75-89.

Singh, Saurabh. (2018). Digital Diplomacy: India's Increasing Digital Footprint.

Stanzel, V., & und Politik-SWP-Deutsches, S. W. (2018). New realities in foreign affairs: Diplomacy in the 21st century.

The Evolution of India's Twitter diplomacy. Hindustan Times. (2021, February 27). Retrieved September 30, 2022, from https://www.hindustantimes.com/opinion/the-evolution-of-india-s-twitter-diplomacy-101614344582598.html

Twitter account of India's top diplomat to the UN hacked. The Wire. (n.d.). Retrieved September 30, 2022, from https://thewire.in/diplomacy/twitter-account-indias-top-diplomat-un-hacked